Look Who's Laughing at
Carpool Tunnel Syndrome!

"While my cartoons are a quick-take on typical family life, Judy Gruen picks up where I left off. **I thank the good Lord she's not drawing a newspaper comic.** Get into this carpool. You'll enjoy the ride."
Bil Keane, creator of "The Family Circus"

"Carpool Tunnel Syndrome will make you laugh with recognition. **Judy Gruen has the same wacky touch as Erma Bombeck.**"
Chris Erskine, columnist, *Los Angeles Times*

"**Terrific!** Every mother will identify...giggling at the hilarious challenges with the good humor of a Judy Gruen."
Diane Medved, author, *Saving Childhood*

"Gruen's book is a funny, stress-reducing antidote to the sheer absurdity of raising kids in today's world."
**Susan K. Perry, Ph.D., author, *Writing in Flow*;
*Fun Time, Family Time***

"The only problem is **you can't read this book in public unless you don't mind people watching you laugh out loud...** Do yourself a favor and get rid of the kids, get some coffee and sit down and read *Carpool Tunnel Syndrome*."
**Mark Schiff, actor, writer, *Mad About You*,
*The Jay Leno Show***

"...humorously saunters through the minefields of motherhood. Readers will smile, chuckle and totally relate to Judy Gruen's love and devotion for family."
Lori Borgman, author, *I Was a Better Mother Before I Had Kids*

"**I was laughing my head off when I read this book.** I have three children of my own so I could relate to Judy's stories. *Carpool Tunnel Syndrome* puts the humor and fun back into parenting. **It's a great book!**"

Rebecca Kochenderfer, editor, *The Education Source*

"Judy Gruen is the mistress of everyday humor of everyday life. I highly recommend *Carpool Tunnel Syndrome* as a book any harried mother, or, indeed, any harried woman, will find filled with familiar situations and full of warmth and wit."

Charlotte Hays, editor, *The Women's Quarterly*

"Reading Judy Gruen's book actually made me entertain, albeit briefly, the notion of wanting four young children in my life, if only for the abundant wellspring of humor that they provide. But then I realized it wasn't the comedic nature of the progeny, but of the parent that counts, and clearly, compared to Gruen, I lack at least one genetic gift: her prodigal sense of perspective. She can turn impatience into generosity, and exhaustion into inspiration, and without the slightest sense of self-pity that so often assumes the bad posture of wit. **If I had to lead the singing through all the campfire circles of child-rearing hell, I'd want Judy Gruen as my head counselor.**"

Michael J. Rosen, editor, *Mirth of a Nation*

"Ms. Gruen captures the joys and trials of motherhood as only an experienced mom could. As a woman trying to balance work and family, I can definitely identify!"

**Pamela Hainlin, president, Mothers & More—
A Network for Sequencing Women
(formerly F.E.M.A.L.E.)**

Carpool Tunnel Syndrome

Motherhood as Shuttle Diplomacy

Judy Gruen

Heaven Ink Publishing   Los Angeles, California

Carpool Tunnel Syndrome:
Motherhood as Shuttle Diplomacy

by Judy Gruen

© 2001 Judy Gruen
ISBN 0-9700737-1-2
Library of Congress Control Number: 00-134243

Published by:
Heaven Ink Publishing
8847 Cattaraugus Avenue
Los Angeles, CA 90034
310-837-2992
1-800-836-1021
heavenink@earthlink.net
www.heavenink.com

10 9 8 7 6 5 4 3 2 1

Cover Illustration: John Caldwell
Cover Design: Rivkah Shifren, Heaven Ink Design
Interior Book Design: Heaven Ink Design
Author Photo: Daryl Temkin Photography

To my mother,

Liebe Rosenfeld

who taught me from an early age that I could

achieve whatever I set out to do.

Her love, encouragement and strength

continue to nourish me...

And in memory of my mother-in-law,

Laura Gruen

who passed away while I was writing this book.

Her warmth and laughter are sorely missed.

Acknowledgments

I want to thank several friends whose suggestions, encouragement, and perceptive editorial and maternal insights were enormously inportant during the drafting of this book. To Linda Abraham, Sharon Altschuler and Beth Firestone, thank you for your time, and for laughing. Author Rochelle Krich, whose mysteries are among the very best, also consistently offered encouragement and technical advice, and I thank her for that. Rivkah Shifren of Heaven Ink Publishing has been a continuous source of valuable insights into the world of publishing. Kudos to Brenda Koplin for her crack proofreading of the final manuscript. Very special thanks to Denise Koek, whose careful attention to comic and linguistic detail have surely enhanced this book. I thank you all for your friendship and enthusiasm.

Certainly, I could not have pursued this project without the support and love of my husband, Jeffrey. You continue to help make my dreams a reality. Finally, I must thank my children, who provide comic fodder for my writing on a daily basis. Despite everything I wrote, you are four fabulous kids, and God has blessed me infinitely by entrusting you to my care. I hope I don't disappoint either you or Him.

— Judy Gruen
Los Angeles
June 2000

Table Of Contents

"My effectiveness as a human being will be a lot greater as a member of Congress than carpooling."
Mary Bono (R-California)

Comment for which Ms. Bono received The Billy Carter Award for Most Amusing Political Relative by *Mother Jones Magazine*. (Following her election, the 38-year-old left her 7- and 9-year-olds in Palm Springs with a nanny.)

....

"Mary Bono is perfect for Congress. In less than three years she's already lost touch with the real world."
Mark Schiff, writer, actor

Chapter 1

Laying My Cards on the Table

It was the kind of typical American dinner scene that would have gotten Norman Rockwell all choked up. My two eldest boys were playing poker under the table, accusing one another of cheating. My 5-year-old daughter reached for the orange juice, accidentally tipping over the soy sauce, which then streamed down her brother's pants. This soy assault sent him into paroxysms of anger and recriminations that would last until breakfast the next morning. Still, practical boy that he is, he returned to the table after changing his pants and resolved to see how much salad he could jam into his mouth with a hand that hadn't seen soap in three days. And my daughter, who has never encountered a topic on which she lacks a definitive opinion, busily chastised the rest of them for their various ill-mannered behaviors.

By this point, everyone's tempers had become far hotter than our neglected dinner.

As I was returning to the table with a mop to clean the spilled soy sauce, and simultaneously attempting to break up the poker game, I began to fear that none of us was playing with a full deck. Just then, my daughter asked me, "Mommy? Why did you ever want to become a mother? It's such hard work!"

"Job security," I answered. "See, honey, even in these days of mega-mergers and corporate buy-outs, my job is safe. I cannot be outsourced or telecommuted. And, though God knows I've tried, I have utterly failed to downsize myself. No other family anywhere in the country would dream of staging a hostile takeover of this conglomerate."

"Huh? I don't understand what any of that means! Say it so I can understand!" she urged, not unfairly.

"Remember, the most important jobs in the world can also be the hardest, like studying for school, going to college, doing a big important project at work. Being a mother is my most important job, even if it is hard sometimes." Gee, I thought, who was this wise and understanding mother speaking? I wanted to get to know her better.

My daughter, a future mother, was listening intently. My salad-gobbling son had moved on to the rice-shoveling competition of the dinner Olympics. Aces were high on the Atlantic City side of the table. With some luck, my husband would be home soon to partake of whatever might be left of dinner.

Really, it's remarkable that women yearn for children and, generally speaking, will feel an aching emptiness without them, despite what our kids put us through! In pregnancy they take over our bodies (mine is still being held hostage somewhere on a fat farm in Eastern Europe). As infants they rob us of sleep and begin the insidious process of stealing our memory cells. As toddlers they ransack the house, decide the walls would look a whole lot better painted with Sassy Cinnamon nail polish, and leave a trail of crumbs everywhere they go, to make sure that we can find them.

It matters not how much they whine, fight, or throw tantrums, we mothers are the ones who see beyond the passion of the moment and believe in our children's talents, strengths, and abilities. We would rather lie down in front of oncoming traffic than let anyone or anything harm our kids.

But still, as my daughter pointed out, this is one helluva job. And we get no benefits! No sick days! Not even stock options for stay-at-home moms, unless you count the chicken stock in the freezer. We are paid in handprints on the refrigerator that say "I Love You a Billion Much" and Mother's Day necklaces made from recycled beads and Cheerios. And we wear them with dignity.

Mothers, be proud of what you do, especially you stay-at-home moms. Your work is irreplaceable.

This book is for all mothers, no matter what other outside work you may do. Because, sisterhood may be powerful, but motherhood is mighty, Herculean, indomitable (though obviously not impregnable!).

So, the next time you are out in public and your child presses an apple core or a mucus-filled tissue into your hand and says, "Here Mommy!" know that she does not simply consider you an ambulatory garbage bin. She loves you! And, even while you pretend to be calm when she whines about your refusal to buy her a $3 helium balloon in the supermarket, and other people are pretending not to look at you and conclude that Joan Crawford was a more affectionate mother than you are, take heart: You are not alone.

Just think, at home later that night, you can pick up this book and read about another mother who has run a mile in your Reeboks.

As a side note, several people who read drafts of this book asked me how much of what I wrote was true. Some of the stories, they said, sounded a little too outrageous to be believed. Believe it! This book is more like a diary than a work of fiction. Admittedly, writing it satisfied a need for both catharsis and, at times, revenge. Almost every story written here is based on my real experiences during nearly a dozen years of motherhood, and most of it happened as I wrote it. (Other than mine, names have been changed to protect the guilty.) Embellishments were small, because as we all know, truth is always stranger than fiction.

(No actual children were harmed in the writing of this book, though dinner often paid the ultimate penalty.)

Chapter 2

How Prepared Are You for Motherhood?

A Quiz with Lots of "None of the Above" Options

Y ou may have noticed that many grown-ups have licenses to do their work. This includes respectable professionals such as hairdressers, who dare not beat anyone's tresses into submission without permission from the state, as well as disreputable individuals, such as attorneys at law. Even the Third World émigré whose name you are getting vertigo trying to read while he hurtles you around the streets of New York City has a license number.

But when was the last time you were in a regular Mom's kitchen and saw on her refrigerator, next to little Montana's drawing of her house and a smiley-face sun, a framed official document indicating that Mom was duly licensed in her state to practice the ancient, at one time revered, art and science of motherhood? Because it smacks of communism, no one has dared try promulgating any form of minimum competency standards for motherhood, which may explain such phenomena as girls named Moonbeam and 3-year-old boys with earrings and haircuts with a spermlike tail in the back. No, developing standards for such a complex enterprise as motherhood would invite a cacophonous debate between the political left and right, between believers and atheists, between carnivores and vegetarians, between people who squeeze the toothpaste from the bottom versus the top. So we are left in the peculiar pickle—metaphorically speaking—of living in a world where an adult may not drive you around the block without a license, but may freely propagate the species, with nary a nod from any authorities. Of course, for the industrious among us, there are always numbers to call to lodge complaints against unfit mothers. These numbers are located in your telephone directory and can be found under the headings "Attorneys at Law" and "Psychotherapists."

I mean, *really*. These days, people spend more time contemplating their Internet access upgrade options than they do considering the future care and feeding of their offspring. Who hasn't been utterly aghast listening to radio shrink shows and hearing grown women discuss their plans to get pollinated by men with whom the only thing they have in common is a weak chin? They may actually devote more time worrying about the feng shui, for goodness' sake, of little Tyler or Brittany's room than they do discussing whether the child should be raised Presbyterian or Wiccan. And marriage, for some, is just too big a commitment.

So, I've developed this handy little quiz (just like in the women's magazines) to help you understand what you are really in for when you take that marvelous, fateful, indelible, breathtaking plunge into motherhood. And while it is very un-PC of me, there are right and wrong answers to this quiz. "Striving" to get the correct answers and lack of self-esteem are no excuse for failing this quiz. However, take heart. If you fail, you can study at your leisure and retake the test anytime. After all, you already paid for the book.

HOW PREPARED ARE YOU FOR MOTHERHOOD?

1. *Which of the following will actually cost the most?*
   a. college education
   b. sports miscellany, such as bouncy balls, basketball nets, bicycle inner tubes, knee pads and annual Little League fees
   c. overdue fines from the library

2. *Which has medical science determined is hardest on the eardrums?*
   a. an off-key high school marching band
   b. fingernails on a chalkboard
   c. an infant with colic

3. *What percentage of food you feed your baby gets into the baby's mouth versus his hair, the floor, or the little Baby Dior jumpsuit?*
   a. 80 percent
   b. 50 percent
   c. 32 percent
   d. none of the above

4. *What is the optimal spacing between children?*
   a. eighteen months
   b. two years
   c. three years
   d. two time zones

5. *Lamaze, Bradley and other natural childbirth systems reduce pain and enhance the exhilarating experience of childbirth.*

    a. true

    b. you've got to be joking

6. *To the nearest trillion dollars, how much do you estimate it will cost to raise your child from birth through college graduation? (Let's assume they're on their own for graduate school.)*

    a. 1 trillion dollars

    b. 4 gazillion dollars

    c. the combined Gross National Product of Germany and Japan

7. *Sibling rivalry can be contained and close fraternal and sisternal relationships can be fostered with proper parental training, patience, and bribery.*

    a. true

    b. what planet did you say you were from?

8. *Useful premotherhood preparation would include work in which fields:*

    a. labor relations mediator

    b. library story-time volunteer

    c. Navy SEAL

    d. origami instructor

    e. bar bouncer

    f. psychologist

    g. New York City cabbie

    h. emergency medical technician

    i. Olympic triathlete

      j. Tupperware salesperson
      k. none of the above
      l. all of the above

9. *The most important thing you should be prepared for before becoming a mother is:*
      a. lack of sleep for approximately two years
      b. lack of privacy for approximately twenty years
      c. perpetual worrying
      d. lack of disposable income
      e. the politics of carpool
      f. none of the above
      g. all of the above

10. *You will never say to your children the things your parents always said to you and those you swore you would never say to your own offspring, such as "Work before fun," "You want to start a dotcom company from your room, fine, but you find the investors," and, "No dessert unless you finish your bok choy."*
      a. false
      b. what was that planet's name again?

11. *A realistic age to expect a child to empty the garbage cans is:*
      a. seven
      b. twelve
      c. thirty-two
      d. never

Well now, even though these questions just barely scratch the surface of all the pre-parenthood information you will need, I don't want to exhaust you just yet. Let's see how you did.

Question 1: *Which of the following will actually cost the most?*

It's logical to have guessed "A," that college education must certainly be more costly than either of the other two categories. But remember, parenthood is full of surprises. In point of fact, if you plan right, college education will cost LESS than either sports miscellany or overdue library fines. Why, in our home, library fines are a line item in the monthly budget. And, while I shouldn't disclose this to the general public, so scandalous did our fines become that my face appeared on the library's Ten Most Wanted List. Don't be shocked if you spend an SUV's worth on library fines, and then you can truthfully plead to your child that you are OUT OF MONEY by the time they get into college. After all, that's why work-study programs were created. Give yourself five points if you guessed "C." Subtract ten points for either "A" or "B."

Question 2: *Which has medical science determined is hardest on the eardrums?*

You may have guessed that the universally reviled sound of fingernails on a chalkboard is correct, and if that was what you picked, feel free to give yourself a point or two (grading is pretty easy on this quiz). And, unless you are watching a rerun of *The Music Man*, you need not fear the auditory threat of a wheezing tuba lumbering your way. So, the correct answer was really "C," a baby with colic. Heartless, you say? You say that colic only lasts a few weeks, a month at most, and that any mom worth her subscription to a parenting magazine should bear with it with perfect equanimity? True. But consider: Colic is a chronic condition that lies dormant for years at a time. Toddler whines and teenage petulance are simply more mature forms of colic, as any seasoned parent can tell you. Give yourself thirty-five points if you figured this out.

Question 3: *What percentage of food you feed your baby gets into the baby's mouth versus its hair, the floor, or its little Baby Dior jumpsuit?*

Idealistic as you are, you may have thought that "A" was correct, and that fully 80 percent of the organically grown and freshly pureed green beans and bananas that you lovingly blended together for your angel actually make it down baby's gullet. If you are this naive, subtract three points from your score. The correct answer is "D," none of the above. Laboratory researchers at the country's leading baby food manufacturers were thrilled to discover that only .00008 percent of baby food makes it past that almost impassable passageway known as "baby's mouth." The other 99.0002 percent can be found on baby's chin, downy hair, nostrils, inside those hard-to-trim fingernails, high chair and anywhere else in the same zip code. Add four points for figuring this out.

Question 4: *What is the optimal spacing between children?*

Penelope Leach, Dr. Laura, and all the rest of the "experts" can dicker all they want about the optimal spacing between children. But the only optimal spacing between children is revealed in answer "D"—two time zones. Preferably, one child should live in Greenwich Mean Time and the other, Central Mountain Time. Getting bedtimes in sync can be tricky, but in my experience, distance only makes the hearts of siblings grow fonder. Give yourself seven points for guessing "D." Subtract eight points for guessing either "A," "B," or "C."

Question 5: *True or False: Lamaze, Bradley and other natural childbirth systems reduce pain and enhance the exhilarating experience of childbirth.*

Oh, the bill of goods we are sold, over and over again throughout our lives! Can you imagine going to the dentist for a root canal and sitting back in the chair, when the dentist looks at you and says, "Have you considered letting me do this with no anesthesia, so that you can fully experience the liberation of those lousy, rotted roots from deep inside your mouth?" Can you imagine a surgeon saying to you, when you arrive for a bypass, "Are you SURE you want to sleep through this? We CAN do this while you're awake, you know, so you can actually feel as I roto-rooter through your chest cavity. How 'bout it? Just remember to breathe deeply and focus on a point deep inside your arteries!" No, of course you can't. People haven't had to voluntarily undergo painful medical procedures without the benefit of anesthesia since the Civil War, for goodness' sakes. But, somewhere back around the time when women thought it good sport to burn their bras in public, they also decided (those who already had their tubes tied) that OTHER women should experience the pain of childbirth—anesthesia-free!

"Natural childbirth is a feminist plot," my friend Sandy said to me as we both waddled down a beachfront boardwalk a dozen years ago in our greatly expectant states. "Don't fall for it," warned she, already a veteran of several births. But did I listen? No! For three of my four childbirth experiences, I was fully, and I do mean FULLY, aware of every excruciating contraction. Since your daughters may read this, and I would never want to discourage them from becoming mothers, I won't even begin to describe the actual birth itself, accompanied as it was by pain generally inflicted only by the most maniacal despots on political prisoners.

Remember, God gave us the brains to invent anesthesia. We should also have the brains to use it. Subtract 163 points if you chose "A." Add forty points if you wisely chose "B."

Question 6: *To the nearest trillion dollars, how much do you estimate it will cost to raise your child from birth through college graduation?*

There are people who, through thrifty measures, have managed to raise a child on a measly trillion dollars. Frankly, I don't know how, other than that they wash their aluminum foil, shop for furniture on the sides of the freeway, and occasionally sneak into soup kitchens. But the mile-high list of other kid-necessities, such as schoolbooks, orthodontic appliances, Popsicles, jump ropes, gerbils, tutors, Star Wars-themed soap and toothpaste, Harry Potter books, well, it just has this darned way of adding up to the kind of numbers that might even give Donald Trump pause. Give yourself two points for "A," four points for "B," and twelve points for "C."

Question 7: *True or False: Sibling rivalry can be contained and close fraternal and sisternal relationships can be fostered with proper parental training, patience, and bribery.*

Please refer back to Question 4 if you need any further clarification on ways to avoid sibling rivalry. I have, by the by, met some extraordinary parents who managed to raise a passel of children who enjoyed a simpatico relationship, at least when company was around. I immediately grabbed these parents by the collar, locked them in a room under the harsh and unforgiving glare of a naked 100-watt bulb, and demanded to know how they did it. They just kind of shrugged, as if it were no big thing, the fact that their kids got along, as if it were as natural as photosynthesis. A lot of help they were.

Oh, by the way, subtract seventeen points if you answered "A" and add nineteen points if you answered "B."

Question 8: *Useful premotherhood preparation would include work in which fields:*

Since women are naturally better at "multitasking" than men, it may explain why we are the mothers and men are the fathers. At any given time, mothers are asked to perform dozens of feats simultaneously. Just the other day, in a span of two minutes, I made pancakes, helped a child calculate the radius of a circle, packed Girl Scout cookies for the troop sale, made dinner plans for my husband and me, screamed at one child for flushing the frog down the toilet, and still answered the phone in a falsely calm and jovial tone. Any experienced mom will instantly recognize that each of the listed occupations would be a tremendous asset to the job of Mother. Give yourself eighty points for "L," all of the above.

Question 9: *The most important thing you should be prepared for before becoming a mother is:*

This question lists only a pitifully few number of the things that will actually come to pass once you are a mother, and they are all true. Add four points if you answered "A," "B," "C," "D," or "E." Subtract 120 points if you thought the answer was "F," and add sixty-eight points for the correct answer, "G."

Question 10: *True or False: You will never say to your children the things your parents always said to you and those you swore you would never say to your own offspring, such as "Work before fun," "You want to start a dotcom company from your room, fine, but you find the investors," and, "No dessert unless you finish your bok choy."*

The answer to this question should be self-evident. Eventually, we ALL become our mothers, even if we spend several years in therapy first. Subtract four points if you chose "A." Add twelve points if you chose "B."

And finally,

Question 11: *A realistic age to expect a child to empty the garbage cans is:*

I know mothers whose children have been grown and out of the house for years and are still waiting for them to take the trash out. However, one mother reported that her son, approaching his twenty-ninth birthday, just up and emptied the garbage—without being asked! So there is always hope.

Now, if your score is a negative number, I'm afraid you have much to learn. You can, however, earn 250 bonus points for each additional copy of this book you purchase and give to a friend. If your answer is a positive integer, congratulations: You seem to have an inkling of what motherhood will be like.

Chapter 3

"Parlez Vous. . .?" Says Who?

When are we going to give this nation's kids a break? The way things are going, our grandchildren will be genetically engineered for hard-wiring to their laptops, cell phones, and pagers. Of course, by that time these will all be the same machine, probably about the size of a credit card. They'll never miss a call, a page, or a stock trade opportunity. They'll be slaves to the world of e-commerce and instant communication, twenty-four/seven. They'll think that "getting away from it all" means an occasional bathroom break. I don't envy what these kids have coming.

Increasingly, parents worry about getting their kids into the right college, the right high school, and even the right preschool. I know of some parents who even draw up resumes of their kids' accomplishments to impress the admissions officers at elite private high schools. Here the kids can tout their achievements in competitive sports, community service, academics, music and other areas. Schools want their students to be well rounded, not just brainy, so a juggernaut of after-school activities becomes de rigueur for this crowd.

Although my children are not fated to study at such elite institutions, I thought it would be fun to draft a résumé of one of my most promising scholars, just to see how he might stack up against the formidable competition. This is what it looked like:

EDUCATION:
- National Achievement Award in Fire-Drill Leadership, signed via computer pen by the president of the United States
- Book reports turned in late only 48 percent of the time
- 68 percent decrease from last year in number of times sent to vice-principal for disruptive behavior (ADD-ADHD label excised from school record as of August)
- Ability to read several-hundred page novels on lap during Social Studies without being caught
- First Prize in essay contest: "If I Were a Crustacean"

COMPETITIVE SPORTS:
- Backyard soccer
- Computer golf
- Poker

FOREIGN LANGUAGES SPOKEN:
- Teen Angst (beginning)
- Mumbling and Belching (conversational)
- Sarcasm (advanced)

COMMUNITY SERVICE:
- Returned stolen candy to shopkeeper in contrite man-

ner when threatened with six-month grounding
- Kicked empty Coke bottle all the way down street to recycling can
- Carried groceries in for neighbor, breaking only three eggs and small bottle of vinegar

MUSICAL INSTRUMENTS PLAYED:
- Armpit
- Spoons

After reviewing the résumé of my wunderkind, I realized that this son did not need the pressure of being thrust into an expensive and snobbish high school. After burning the document, I gave no more thought to grasping beyond our educational or financial stratum.

But I feel sorry for kids whose parents aren't as practical as I am. These days, even babies are under pressure to perform, and that's before they're even born. Increasingly, busy professional moms are demanding that their babies be conceived and born according to a timetable. Women used to try to time their pregnancies to vacations ("Just one more December in Aspen, and THEN I'll get pregnant!"). Now, they are trying to squeeze in a conception sometime after the semi-annual shareholders' meeting but before the new product launch in Korea. No kidding, more and more career women are huddling over their Palm Pilots and having conversations like this:

"Okay, Shelly, you're up for the next pregnancy, but I hope you aren't planning to be on maternity leave when we start the Burly Billfold Company ad campaign. You know how testy their people can be, and it's your account."

"No sweat, Donna. The campaign launches in August, so

I've already penciled in 'conception' on my calendar for July 15. Assuming I can get pregnant by September, I'll be at work through the important national and international conventions and still be back for the next time the Burly Billfold people come to town. Then, according to our schedule, you'll get pregnant sometime in March or April, and deliver no later than mid-November, otherwise I may get stuck with that blasted 'Fun With Fiberglass' campaign."

"Let's just hope the babies cooperate!"

"That's for sure! We've worked too hard to mess up such a great work schedule!"

I can't speak for other ova, but if I were a party to that conversation, I think I'd hold on for dear life to Ms. Fallopian and refuse to take that fateful slide toward certain deadline pressure.

And once these babes are born, the pressure continues to mount—especially where their educations are concerned. Many parents apparently believe that if their infants aren't speaking Berber by the time they're through with Gerber, their prospects for a successful seven-figure career may be shot.

Here's a case in point. A reporter for the *Wall Street Journal* divulged (with no embarrassment, mind you) her own experience signing up her 6-month old daughter for a sell-out Spanish language course near her home in Manhattan. The thinking is that even though the students are in more of a drool mode than a speech mode, immersion in a foreign language will somehow ratchet up their IQs. The language lessons they hear will lie dormant for years, and suddenly, when you least expect it, the kid will begin reading Plato's Republic in Greek.

Tantalized by this prospect of creating Einsteinian minds, Manhattanite moms crammed enough strollers into the school's hallway to choke the Lincoln Tunnel. The event was strictly CRO (crawling room only). The course instructor lauded these forward-thinking parents for anteing up the big bucks for the class. And I do mean big bucks. For this amount of money, the toothless throng could have earned several credits at Columbia University and been well on their way to a law degree. I wondered how the teachers of these language classes could keep a straight face, declining verbs to a roomful of tots whose most recent accomplishment was rolling over and sleeping a six-hour stretch. But hey, isn't this what a free-market economy is all about?

The moms who packed this room weren't fazed by the fact that their babies appeared more interested in snack time at their breasts than in conjugating verbs. Studies had proven to the moms' satisfaction that messages drilled into babies' heads even before their skull bones have fused completely are embedded more thoroughly than the cookies the babes will one day cram into Mommy's computer hard drive.

I thought this whole setup was a riot. I mean, if this education theory is true, and babies do internalize messages drilled into them for years afterward, why not teach them more practical expressions and concepts?

If it were my class, I'd skip the foreign languages and get right to the nitty gritty.

"You will take out the garbage cans every Tuesday night," I would say, clearly enunciating each word to my round little charges.

"You must not question Mommy or Daddy's authority on any subject, ever," I would say to the room full of tabula rasas, who were busy filling their diapers.

"You must pay for your own automobile insurance if you intend to drive a car," I would say sweetly, walking around the room and passing out a teething toy to an especially alert listener.

"No, you may not go to the Chew DoggyDog concert tonight," I would soothe, gently patting the irresistibly fat thigh of one scholar and handing her a rattle.

"If Cro-Magnon man was able to invent cutlery using only a stone and a spear, you, too, can use a fork," I would address a student with a pate of peach fuzz.

All in all, I think I could come up with a terrific curriculum for babies. I would teach them that the keys to popularity in school are hospital corners on their beds and an aversion to any movie starring Brad Pitt. I would charge a lot less than these chichi language labs, and parents would thank me for it one day when their kids are teenagers. I can just picture it now:

"Gosh, Sam, what's wrong? Everything okay at home?"

"No, it's not! Macallister is on the phone again speaking Dutch with his girlfriend, and I can't find my Dutch-English dictionary to figure out what they're saying. How I rue the day when I signed him up for that infant language immersion program! That's where he met little Brittany Madonna, and they've been speaking Dutch ever since!"

"Gee, I'm sorry about that, Sam. I hope they're not planning another hacking job at the CIA. That was quite a sticky situation last time around, wasn't it?"

"You're not kidding. Count your blessings that Cheyenne only speaks English. By the way, where is Cheyenne?"

"You must have just missed her. She took out the garbage and then went to deliver meals to some shut-ins."

The way I figure it, there's a wide world of opportunity in the children's education market. For older children, I'm developing a whole "continuing education" program. Kids can apply their continuing education credits toward purchases at electronics stores, later bedtimes, and other perks. And, since no one else seems to be teaching these skills, I plan to capture the market in a little-practiced, anachronistic field: civility.

For the beginning level, my course list includes the following:

- "Majestic Mastication: Learning to Chew with Your Mouth Closed"
- "Napkins: Not Just a Table Ornament Anymore"
- "Angels with Dirty Faces: Introduction to Soap and Washcloths"
- "Right Foot, Wrong Shoe: Don't Trip on the Road to Success"

and

- "Meet the Hamper: Target Practice for Fun and Profit"

For intermediate students, I'm working on the following course material:

- "Getting Beyond 'Yeah': Techniques for Multi-Syllabic Conversation"
- "Chicken Soup for the Bowl: Learning to Ladle, Serve and Perform Other Necessary Functions at Dinnertime"
- "The Seven Habitats of Highly Effective People: The Video Arcade and Shopping Mall Are Not Among Them"

and

- "MTV: You Don't Have to End Up This Way"

Finally, for really advanced students:

- "The Bucks Stop Here: Get a Job!" (This class is open to all girls but only boys who have first completed the intro courses, "Toilet Flushing for Dummies" and "The Fly Starts Here: Zip Up Before You Zip Out.")

- "Napkins: Still Not Just a Table Ornament"
- "If You Want a Hurricane Named After You, Don't Clean Up Your Room"
- "Parents and Lines of Credit: How to Tell the Difference"

and

- "You May Be from Mars or Venus Originally but You've Gotta Live on Planet Earth Now"

Now, as for teaching babies Spanish, many parents have accomplished the same thing for a lot less money. How? They go to work, and leave their little pumpkins at home with Spanish-speaking housekeepers, who chatter to them lovingly all day long and allow them to eavesdrop on their favorite Spanish-language soap operas. Believe me, these kids know their *leche* from their *jugo* before they cut their first teeth. Want your baby to learn French? Vietnamese? Croat? No problem! Just find a housekeeper or nanny of a different ethnicity. Hey, America's the world's "salad bowl" of multiculturalism. Let's make it work for us.

I'm not totally cynical. In fact, I do believe that exposure to foreign languages and even classical music helps develop critical thinking skills. I have purchased and played many of these titles, including "The Itsy-Bitsy Spider Went Down Schubert's Spout," "Mozart for Mammals," and "Peek-a-Boo with Pachobel." At dinner I tried to create a harmonious environment and promote critical thinking skills by installing a CD player in the kitchen, where we often play classical music during meals. Unfortunately, in my case, the tapes worked too well. My kids' ability to think critically, particularly regarding their siblings, is sharper than a pair of stiletto heels. Perhaps I overdid it.

"Isn't this a beautiful adagio?" I ask at dinnertime.

"Eee-yew! She's wiping her feet with the dish towel! You're disgusting!"

"Yeah? What about you? You haven't washed your hands for a million billion years! And why did you take the last pickle? You're so selfish!"

"Listen! Here comes the intermezzo!"

"Mom! He dropped his chicken on the floor and picked it up and ATE IT! Everyone at this table is disgusting except me."

"Ahh! What synchronous execution!"

This just goes to prove two things, in my opinion. First, that it's no coincidence that "Happy Hour" at bars is usually between five and seven in the evening, when moms across America typically serve dinner to their children. Because as everyone knows, there are no children allowed in bars. Clearly, the whole concept of "Happy Hour" had to have been invented by a mom who somehow ducked out of dinner duty one night and found herself in a local watering hole, blissfully alone with her thoughts and a margarita. Thus, another sacred cultural institution was born, and we undoubtedly have a woman to thank for it.

The second thing my example proves is that even when it comes to dining ambiance, such as classical music, you can have too much of a good thing. I'm just glad I didn't heap foreign language lessons on top of it.

Chapter 4

Things That Go Beep in the Night

It's 1:47 a.m., and I'm on a stakeout in my bedroom. Not for anything exciting or relevant, like the cops out somewhere in the city, smoking out a drug dealer at a cheap motel. There, the cops will eventually burst from their unmarked squad car, guns trained on the perp, and capture their quarry. And the city will have one less threat to its peace and tranquility. No, the similarity between the cops and me ends with the fact that we are both waiting silently in the dark, wish we were sleeping, and, perhaps, that we would each appreciate a doughnut and coffee.

My stakeout has no consequences for the safety of my fair city, but has enormous consequences for my mental stability. See, I am lying in wait until the next time that my 7-year-old son's Giga-pet unleashes its next set of annoying beeps, which rudely woke me and gave me a frightening feeling of solidarity with deranged postal workers.

This toy, a $5.99 glorified key chain that gained wild and undeserved popularity among the ten-and-under age group, offers children the conceit that they are actually taking care of a small and helpless creature, such as a baby.

The Giga-pet beeps when it (you should pardon the expression) "poops," "sleeps," or "is hungry." In theory, this is a harmless toy, but these beeps are bad news.

The Giga-pet first announced itself at 1:45 a.m., just long enough to have dragged me from a pleasant dream and to have realized that I had to get out from under my cozy blanket to find the damned thing. I wait in darkness, not wanting to wake my sleeping husband, and grope around in the dark for this little, loathsome toy.

When it beeps again, I lunge toward the dresser, from where the beeps seemed to emerge. I feel around on top of the dresser, like an investigator sleuthing in Braille, but only find some folded clothing, miscellaneous bills, and my keys. Then, the toy shuts up.

Feeling monumentally frustrated, I think, "Hey, this isn't my doing. My son left this here. HE should find it." After all, I thought, if the kid wants to feel like a parent, let him wake up with his baby in his room, where he is free to feed it, change it or smash it in a zillion pieces, as I plan to do as soon as I find it. This really was a '90s kind of toy, though: Press a button, and voilà! Problem solved. Hardly a real training ground for parenthood.

I decide that I will waste no more time feeling the fool, squandering precious sleep in this absurd quest. I march down the hall to my son's room and get into his chubby, sleeping face. I try not to think about the fact that I have never, ever had to do anything like this in my twelve years of motherhood.

"Hey!" I shout, though in a whisper. "Did you leave your

STUPID LITTLE TOY, the one that BEEPS, in my room today?"

Now my son is the one awakened from a good dream and caught in a bad one. His eyes widen, and, being the clever child that he is, my son realizes that this is not a purely social visit. He nods his head, slowly.

"Well, it's BEEPING NOW, and I CAN'T FIND IT," I snarl. "Get out of bed and FIND IT before I get REALLY MAD!"

My child, who had been in deep REM mode thirty seconds before, sprints out of bed and into my room. "I think I left it on your bed," he says, somehow miraculously remembering to whisper. This boy's normal speaking pitch is loud enough to project throughout Dodger Stadium. Living with him is like living in "Surround Sound." He starts feeling around the bed covers, and on the sheets.

"It's not there, I would have found it already," I hiss. "Keep looking."

I stand sentry as he darts around, quickly finding it on the little table next to the television. "Found it!" he says, no doubt relieved that Mommy Dearest may soon leave him alone.

"Get it out of here," I snap through gritted teeth, following him back to his room to make sure that this little electronic irritant does not darken my doorway again, at least for the rest of the night. He holds the Giga-pet in hand, while I work very hard to prevent myself from snatching the toy away and taking a hammer to it. In his room, I open his Special Drawer, where my son keeps precious items, including several dozen baseball and basketball cards, some rocks, a baby tooth still awaiting its payoff from a delinquent Tooth Fairy, and a plastic brontosaurus, and shove the Giga-pet in the back. I slam the drawer shut.

"If I hear this beeping again, EVER, you will never see it again," are my soothing maternal words of farewell.

It's one thing to waken in the middle of the night to care for an actual human being, which, as a mother, I have done thousands of times. My husband and I have given up years of sleep to feed, change, comfort, soothe, clean, administer medication and otherwise tend to the needs of our real-live children. While this was exhausting, at least it had a purpose. But this? To lie in wait for a cheap battery-operated import that our trading partners from the Far East have dumped on American soil? You gotta be kidding.

The Night of the Beeps got me to thinking about how much I always disliked electronic toys. I wondered if perhaps they weren't a form of revenge on the part of passive-aggressive grandparents getting back at their grown children for all the *tzuris* the kids caused while growing up.

"Oh, get a load of this, Mildred," a grandfather might say to his wife in fiendish delight, demonstrating a particularly obnoxious electronic alphabet game at the local toy emporium. And, perhaps not even realizing his stream of consciousness train of thought, he might say, "Remember all those times Sheila would whine when we wouldn't give her an ice cream after school? Say, why don't we give this toy to little Aubrey?"

Or, to give the benefit of the doubt, since grandparents are generally wonderful people and I would hate to denigrate such a valuable and cheap source of babysitters, maybe the grandparents simply don't know the powerful influence of these electronic toys. They may truly think those things are something really swell, a way to stimulate the mind and encourage learning. They don't realize that these same toys can also twist their adult children's minds in ways that only angel dust might have done to them twenty-five years earlier, namely, drive them to the brink of lunacy. I suspect, however, that grandparents DO know how torturous the games can be.

Why else would they drop the gifts off for the grandkids and then claim that they "can only stay a minute"? I mean, how many rounds of golf can you play in a week? Hmmmm?

My generation didn't have electronic toys, generally speaking. The most sophisticated toy I remember was a Suzy Homemaker, a little oven that really baked tiny cakes and muffins. Can you imagine such a sexist, gender-specific gadget making it to market today? The mind reels at the thought of the social upheaval that would follow: University students would chain themselves to the women's studies departments (not a bad idea, if you think about it). The EEOC and many other alphabet organizations would file lawsuits. Hollywood stars, always an entertaining source of cutting-edge sociological thought, would testify at specially called congressional hearings. Postal rates would increase. Anyway, when I was a young girl, the Suzy Homemaker was breathtakingly sophisticated, what with its little light bulb inside and real heat threatening to burn a hole in my bedroom carpet. Otherwise, we played board games, jumped rope, skated (on skates that had actual metal wheels), and did other low-tech stuff.

My theory about the passive-aggressive grandparents may explain why most of these electronic toys are purchased by the grandparents and not by the actual parents, who know better than to bring into their homes—on purpose—a thing that will incessantly announce letters, animal sounds, or brief portions of songs. Over and over and over again. Gramps and Gran aren't in the house when little Chester keeps pounding the same button, relentlessly, despite the fact that he has his choice of twenty-four or forty-eight or 159 other buttons to choose from. Trust me: If mommy or daddy is in the room, the only button that Chester will press is the one that goes:

"OldMcDonOldMcDonOldMcDonOLDMCDONOLD

MCDONald had a farm, EiEiO!"

Or,

"Blue? THAT'S RIGHT! Blue? THAT'S RIGHT! Blue? THAT'S RIGHT! Blue? THAT'S RIGHT! Blue? THAT'S RIGHT! BLUE? THAT'S RIGHT!!!"

Fortunately, many of these electronic toys have the life span of a goldfish. When their batteries mercifully run out, you can honestly tell your child that you don't know of many stores that sell the replacement batteries, which are often the size of a tiny button and have obscure names, such as G to the ninth power.

Me, I never, ever give an electronic toy as a gift. At least, not to kids whose parents I like.

Chapter 5

Tanks But No Tanks

I think I finally understand why animal rights groups don't make waves about pet fish. I now understand this because we recently acquired a tank full of them. Frankly, they're a pain in the neck.

How is it that a ten-gallon aquarium now has squatting rights on what had been our only remaining uncluttered bathroom counter? Sure, the kids had tried to strongarm us into getting them a pet before, but we had always rebuffed their efforts. We liked the idea of pets, theoretically, but the thought of extra living things around the house that needed cleaning, chasing and algae-purging stopped us cold.

Eventually I caved in, and regretted it immediately. One afternoon, when I picked up my daughter from a school carnival, she ran over to me excitedly holding up that dreaded plastic bag with the lone goldfish in it, saying, "Look Mommy! I won a GOLDFISH! For FREE!"

I decided to be a good sport.

"How wonderful!" I said, deciding that this was my "golden" opportunity to show the kids that I wasn't so rigid about pets after all. "We'll stop by Pets-A-Rama on the way home and buy a nice big tank and some friends for him."

"Mommy! She's a girl fish, not a boy fish!"

"Yes, fine, we'll buy some friends for HER." My boys were just as eager to finally join the ranks of Pet Owners.

An hour later, this "free" fish had set me back $97.86, and I was not exactly oozing enthusiasm about this adventure anymore. Although technically too young to have a "senior moment," I could not recall from my own childhood that goldfish needed so many accoutrements. I only agreed to tote home the fish because I thought it was low maintenance. But, like most other things from my past, even goldfish had become complicated. When I brought my own plastic bag home from the school carnival, I remember my mom just pouring it into an empty mayonnaise jar that she filled with water. End of story. We fed the fish till it died, which didn't take long, and then moved on with our lives. So when, in the intervening years, did it become necessary to also buy a sprawling aquarium, a filter, five pounds of colorful gravel, water conditioner, and plastic plants? To create ambiance? Since when do fish need ambiance? And get this—they also needed tablets with a name like "Calming Crustacean Chews" to relax the fish when they were "stressed."

"How do I know when the fish are suffering from 'stress'?" I asked Julius, the patient custodian of the Pets-A-Rama fish department.

"Sometimes you can just tell," he said with heartbreaking sincerity.

I made a mental note to monitor the Federal Reserve, and

keep track of the next spike in interest rates. For all I knew, this might overstress my goldfish.

It soon became clear that spending a C-note to create the perfect aquatic environment did not yield the desired result. Because, even with all this junk, goldfish still have the average lifespan of a soufflé. Even as we were still rinsing the stupid aquarium gravel (because you could not just put UNTREATED gravel in the fish tank, a fact you would know if you watched the instructional video and read the booklet that you also had to buy at Pets-A-Rama) and waiting for our new water to "settle" to just the right temperature, which we gauged with the aquarium's stick-on thermostat, my daughter's goldfish had the nerve to die. Was it the excitement that killed her? Was it the stress of realizing she had come to live in a household that was not, shall we say, as serene as an ashram? Of course, we'll never know, but my daughter's wails of sorrow and heart-wrenching agony were probably already killing the dear departed's "friends" still waiting patiently in their Baggies to swim into their new lives in the big tank.

The situation remained critical the rest of the day. When one child accused my daughter of being more broken up over the demise of her goldfish than she had been when Great-uncle Izzy had passed on, the entire house was convulsed with acrimony. Sentimental girl that she is, my daughter recovered from her bereavement after being promised a new fish the next day.

Things seemed to move along swimmingly over the next few days. I mentioned to a friend that we had bought an aquarium, and he laughed. "You should have saved your money. I would have gladly given you ours. Nothing but trouble, those fish. Pretty to look at, but that algae buildup! Really gross. And the kids get so upset when the fish die. The only fish worth having in the house are dead ones, filleted, sautéed and slathered with dill sauce."

"We've only lost one fish so far," I said, defensively. "And between the filter and the algae eater, I'm sure we'll keep our tank clean." My friend could not suppress his smile. His greater experience unnerved me. I wanted to prove him wrong, and show him that Team Gruen was capable of keeping five lousy goldfish alive. After all, we were raising children, weren't we? Weren't children more complex life forms than fish?

Our fish seemed a friendly enough bunch, and though they didn't wag their fins with delight when they saw us, at least they didn't cause any further disasters.

Until the following week. That's when I felt the full impact of my friend's knowing smile. One night, a hairline fracture in the bottom of the tank ruptured, flooding the floor and several cabinet drawers, ruining several boxes of bandages and medications in the process.

This was not how I had planned to spend the midnight hour, cleaning up and caretaking our now homeless fish.

In the morning, I made another trip to Pets-A-Rama to get a replacement tank. Why was it that every time I went in there they told me about another "must have" for fish sustenance? This time, it was a heater. Next time, it will probably be a Ph.D. in marine biology.

And, despite the new tank, the filter, water conditioner, "Calming Crustacean Chews," ambient plants, and their own personal trainer, our fish remained contemptuous of our efforts to keep them alive. One morning soon after this episode, one son woke me up with the news that all our remaining fish were dead.

"Great. Just our luck," I said. "They probably belonged

to one of those suicidal religious cults in Africa. Go flush them down the toilet."

I got out of bed and padded toward the bathroom, where I discovered that the reports of fishes' demise had been somewhat exaggerated. The algae eater had certainly died, no doubt from overeating. One of his buddies also seemed to be "aquatically challenged," but the rest appeared to be alive, though admittedly in need of life support. My daughter was scooping up her live replacement fish and was about to flush it down the toilet as well.

"Wait! Don't do that!" I said. "It's still alive."

"I don't want it anymore," she said. "I'm sending it back to the ocean."

"Honey, it won't go back to the ocean if you do that. You will kill it. Put it back in the tank. Anyway, at this rate it'll probably die by lunchtime."

"Fine with me."

"There's simply no point to having a relationship with a fish," observed my philosophical 10-year-old.

I was pretty peeved. For a supposedly low-maintenance, "free" pet, I had spent the better part of a week and half my grocery money on the care, feeding and replacement of these ridiculous fish. This didn't even count the money I had spent to replace the medicines and bandages lost in The Great Flood. What a mistake these fish had been! We would have had more fun if we had brought home the Loch Ness monster. I went back to Pets-A-Rama, feeling like a fishwife.

"Excuse me," I said to Julius, "but you keep selling me fish that die. Don't you guys have some kind of warrantee on these things? I've bought strawberries with longer expiration dates than your fish. Sometimes they keel over even before we make it home."

"Well, I don't have any problem with MY fish," he said. "Are you sure you're not overfeeding them?"

"We feed them twice a day, just like it says on the package."

"No, no, no! You're only supposed to feed them twice a *week*. No wonder they're dying."

"What!" I was outraged. "How'm I supposed to know that, when the directions say twice a day on the package?"

"They just want to sell more fish food, that's all. Hey, I woulda toldja if you'd've asked me," Julius said.

I thrust a new, blue, algae-resistant plastic plant at him. "And YOU just want to sell more fish! That would explain why every time I'm in here, I get another piece of the puzzle about how to keep these stupid, ungrateful, slimy, smelly creatures alive!"

I put back the new plastic plant, realizing that I would no longer be a willing dupe in this aquatic Ponzi scheme. I saw it all clearly now, far more clearly than anyone could see into our three-week-old algae-ridden aquarium/hospice. No wonder that Pets-A-Ramas were popping up faster than popcorn all over town! Who could keep up with the demand for new fish to replace those that had already gone to that big freshwater tank in the sky?

And to think that I had withheld a puppy from my kids! A puppy, who would have showered us with affection... wagged his tail with excitement when he saw us, bathed us with his doggy-breath love and gratitude simply because we took care of him! With fish, the biggest satisfaction we ever got was seeing that they weren't floating at the top of the tank in the morning! Okay, so maybe a puppy would cause a little mischief, maybe chew up a shoe or two, but at least he'd last longer than a bag of salad in the refrigerator. I looked longingly over at the puppies in their glass cases. They were romping around so charmingly, their big eyes so frisky and inviting...maybe I could talk my husband into getting one.

After all, even the most rambunctious puppy couldn't be as much trouble as these scaly little goldfish.

Could it?

Chapter 6

How Green Was My Checkbook

I once had a dream that I had morphed into an ATM machine. And in this dream, my kids stood in line before me, each waiting impatiently to punch in their PIN numbers so that they could extract steady wads of cash from my innards. Because I had not been programmed with voice capabilities, I could not say, "Lost your science book again, pal?" Nor could I even ask, "When will I get it back?" But I suppose even a brainless hunk of steel would know better than to ask a stupid question like that. My only consolation, as I spat out twenties the way my children spat out asparagus, was the small service fee I got to charge for each withdrawal—leaving me only enough pocket change for a non-gourmet cup of coffee.

Dreams do imitate life, because as all moms and dads know, kids are financial leeches. This isn't really their fault. After all, we brought them into the world, and according to the Helsinki accords, we are obligated to provide food, shelter, clothing, medical care, and Dopey-mon cards. But where is it written that we must also ante up for ballet instruction, tai kwon do lessons, Little League sports, incessant computer game upgrades, drama camp, in-line skates, bicycles, ortho-donture, and, during the summer, a steady infusion of ice cream?

Lots of kids have grown up just fine without these "extras." Take orthodonture, for example. I think you could make a mighty good argument that having less than perfect choppers is no excuse for lack of achievement later in life. I mean, we all can't have teeth like Julia Roberts. And who would want to? You can't even look at her without ultraviolet sunglasses. But speaking of toothsome celebrities, just look at supermodel Lauren Hutton. Apparently, her parents weren't worried about that gap between her front teeth, and they were correct. Maybe a couple of kids made fun of her when she was a child, but I bet they stopped laughing some time in the next twenty years when her gappy smile graced the cover of every other magazine that arrived at their miserable mobile homes. And even when she had enough money to arrange to have her two front teeth meet each other, she didn't! That's what I call rugged individualism.

That said, I can't really cut corners here, since my kids' permanent teeth have a tendency to grow in at right angles from one another. But in our orthodontist's office, a wall full of satisfied patients' photos reveals that many of them are adults. So, I figure, anyone with kids whose teeth aren't growing in a devil-may-care fashion might want to consider letting them pay for their own mouth full of metal when they're all grown up. You'd better believe that when the kids are shelling out the dough, you won't have to remind them to wear their neck gears at bedtime.

Parents have to economize somewhere, since kids suck the money out of us like a force field in a science fiction thriller. Frequently, these are for expenses we can't anticipate. Two of my boys—on separate occasions, and apparently with no collusion between them—have cracked my minivan windshield. One really used his head. Not metaphorically, by thinking up a way to break it, but literally, by butting against it very hard. The other boy cracked the windshield with his own bare 4-year-old hands, while trying to pry off the rear-view mirror. Since boys of all ages can't seem to resist a good demolition, each boy was pretty pumped up by his achievement. Me, I was out another 250 notes of legal tender to the local auto glass company. The guys there thought my kids were the best thing to come along since glass tinting. Whenever I came in, they made sure to fuss over my "cute" kids.

"They're available to rent on the weekends," I said. "Here's a coupon good for this month only: Rent one, get the second one free."

Suddenly, the mechanics backed away toward their bays, giving me a strange, frightened look.

Boys and girls will ring up different types of expenses. Girls will wrest more money out of you for clothing, hair accoutrements, plastic surgery, and long-distance telephone calls. Boys will cost substantially more in breakage, hospital emergency room visits, and tennis shoes large enough to fit NBA guards. Once, after having replaced another window (this time in the house) that the boys had shattered playing ball, I sighed to a family friend, "I wish they sold some kind of insurance against this type of damage."

"They do," he said tartly. "It's called birth control."

Since the children were all accomplished facts by that time, his comment was of no help. I decided, therefore, to try to staunch the geyser of greenbacks shooting out of our wallets and into the atmosphere. But how? I grabbed a magazine that had been lying around featuring a woman who, through meticulous menu planning and coupon clipping, spent only $2.47 a week feeding her family of four. The article claimed that this titan of thrift had managed to save so much on groceries that she was able to purchase a home! I tried her gambit once and saved 95 cents, but it meant buying one of those brands of gluey organic baking soda toothpastes that nobody liked. Fighting years of frugality, I didn't even wait till it got crusty before I threw it out.

Actually, these coupon come-ons hoodwink a lot of people. Just think: Is it really worth anyone's time to save a buck on a certain kind of orange juice, but only if you mark your calendar for three weeks from Thursday between midnight and 8:00 a.m., when the coupon is honored? Who really wants to soak the label off a mayonnaise jar just so you can fill out the attached survey on cholesterol, which nets you a 50-cents-off coupon after you mail it back in? I don't know how that coupon-clipping house-buying lady did it, but I wasn't having any of it.

I thought the way to go was to shop at one of those member-only warehouse stores, where the savings were as substantial as the containers of food they sold. Luckily, one had just opened up near me, so I ran right over and plunked down $40 for the privilege of pushing around a shopping cart the size of a John Deere tractor. Once inside Big Food-A-Plenty, I didn't know where to begin, but I had to think fast to dodge the forklift heading my way. The place was a supermarket on steroids, eight times larger than the Houston Astrodome, and there was nothing it didn't sell: pasta by the pound, socks by the score, pickles in profusion. Whatever you wanted to buy at

Big Food-A-Plenty, you had better like it, because it only came in multiples. Enthused with my plan to save my family money, I filled my cart with impunity.

Once in the mile-long line to pay, I realized with horror that the store only took cash, checks and an obscure credit card issued by a bank I'd never heard of in Nebraska. My kids see to it that I never have more than $20 dollars in cash at any given time, and my checking account had only enough to cover my twin-pack of gallon-sized ketchup. Exasperated, I asked a clerk to hold my cart while I went to the bank to withdraw enough cash to save my family money.

I found, however, that this kind of economy has its own costs. For one thing, I managed to ring up $387.61 while trying to conserve our financial resources. (Good thing I resisted the temptation to buy that telescope they had on sale for only $229—regularly $350!) For another, I wasn't sure if anyone would like the new "Roughage-Os" cereal I found, but I hoped so, since it only came in an eight-pound box.

When I got home, I shouted "Groceries! Come and help, everyone!" a plea that, like so many others, fell on hearing-impaired ears. I dragged them, one by one, to the van, pointed to my haul, and said, "Get a move on. I'll break my back lifting that twenty-five-pound bag of brown rice by myself. Here, each of you take one side, and carry it like a couch, with one of you backing into the house with it. That way it will fit in the doorway."

"But Mom, we don't like brown rice!" cried one.

"Look, I'm saving money here, and this whole bag was only six bucks. Besides, brown rice has many more nutrients than white rice."

"Hey, look at this! Mom got a box of forty-four Kit-Kat bars and a box of a 120 waffles! Thanks, Mom!"

"Stop tearing into that box," I said. "No one gets a Kit-Kat until everything is brought into the house and you eat at least four pounds of rice."

"Why do we need twelve blue towels?" another asked, carrying in both the towels and a twin-pack of gallon-sized mystery brand hair conditioner made with chunks of real sea kelp.

"They only sold them in dozens. They'll keep," I said, perhaps too defensively.

"Someone help me with this," my daughter said, pulling ineffectually on the plastic handle of a 30-pound tub of laundry detergent whose instructions were written in Armenian. "I can't lift it."

"Of course not. It weighs almost as much as you do. Boys, take that from her."

"Mom, just where do you think we're going to keep all this stuff? The pantry's kind of full, isn't it?"

"You don't know the meaning of the word," I said, hefting a crate of toilet paper into the house and, looking around, realizing it would have to serve as a small end table in the living room for the time being.

"Who's going to eat all this salad? Are we having company for dinner?" another son asked as he hauled a five-pound bag of prewashed salad greens and a flat of tomatoes into the kitchen.

Looking around the kitchen, I realized my son's idea had potential. If I kept shopping at Big Food-A-Plenty, I would need to spend at least another $400 dollars to buy a second refrigerator. Otherwise, I'd have to revert to the wasteful habit of buying eggs by the dozen, when they were so much cheaper to buy sixty at a time. But until then, I just had one fridge. And despite my credentials as a Gold Medal finalist in the "cram more food into the fridge" decathlon, I couldn't imagine how we would keep today's purchases from spoiling. Besides, I had also snapped up five incredibly cheap smoked fish, 600 paper plates and almost as many napkins, 350 Styrofoam cups and eight bags of plastic cutlery. If I cooked a few pounds of the brown rice or pasta, we could host a block party.

When my husband came home, he was more than a little surprised to see us all on the front lawn, eating at the picnic table, with a sign hanging from it that said "Free Food!" My kids and I had set up a buffet of an all-you-can-eat salad bar, smoked fish, the infamous brown rice (which brought the macrobiotic neighbors out in droves) and waffles for dessert.

"What's going on here?" he said. He noticed that our buffet was rapidly being depleted, and, in a survival-of-the-fittest mode, started filling his own plate before we'd answered his question.

"Mom went shopping at the Big Food-A-Plenty today," explained our daughter, "and we didn't have room to keep it all. But she saved us a LOT of money."

Chapter 7

Pair of Dice, Lost

*or, Why Your Sons Play Like
Cain and Abel While
Your Daughters Play House*

*"Cain spoke with his brother Abel.
And it happened when they were in the field,
that Cain rose up against his brother
Abel and killed him."*
(Genesis 4:8)

Now on the face of it, this may not seem the most auspicious introduction to the institution of brotherhood. I mean, here they are, the very first brothers in recorded history, and what happens? Even with the whole world to themselves, Cain decides that his enormous garden just ain't big enough for the two of them, and makes good on his threat to become an only child again.

According to the Bible, Cain was jealous because Abel one-upped him in the Divine Offerings department. But frankly, any old excuse would have done.

"Abel! Have you seen my basketball cards?" Cain may have demanded.

"Nah. I've been out here all morning, gathering barley."

"Well, how about my dice? I bet you took them!"

"Dice?" Abel thinks. "Yeah, I played with them, but I'm sure I put them back in your room. By the way, did you know you have a knife just lying around on your dresser? You oughta put that thing away before someone gets hurt."

Like many fraternal pranks, Cain's assault on his brother could have been a desperate plea to get his mother's attention. Maybe he had said, "Mom, when are you going to finish up with that snake-oil salesman in the backyard? You said you'd take me to Clay Pots 'R Us!" But perhaps, like many busy mothers, she had said, "Just a MINUTE! Besides, you haven't finished your threshing, have you?" Or, perhaps Eve was on the telephone with someone selling mutual funds. Clearly, some biblical commentators might lay the blame for this first instance of fratricide at the bare feet of Eve, as if she didn't have enough problems already. Let's face it, how would YOU like to be responsible for introducing the concept of pain in childbirth into the world? Hmmm? Never again would the choice between Pippins or Granny Smiths seem as innocent.

And let's be honest: If the Bible is any blueprint at all, one can't help but be a little worried about the prospects of brothers ever getting along. Noah's sons got into a serious tiff as soon as the ark landed. Jacob's sons hatched a plan to dispatch their brother Joseph, and sold him into slavery to the first itinerant spice traders who happened along. And on and on.

Still, the way I look at it, the story of Cain and Abel should be reassuring. After all, if you have sons, and they only get into the occasional knock-down, drag-out, a bloody nose or chipped tooth now and again, and no one gets sold into slavery, you're probably doing okay as a mother. The Bible's giving us fair warning: "Listen, folks," it is saying, "brothers naturally want to kill each other. If yours don't, congratulations. Just expect a lot of visits to the emergency room as they grow up."

Brothers are funny guys. One summer, when my oldest had been at sleep-away camp for three weeks, I took his next younger brother to the orthodontist. Now, with only eighteen months between them, and personalities as different as Groucho Marx may have been from his long-lost brother, Karl, I expected the younger son to have loved this respite from being the repository of every caustic remark and baseball his brother could hurl at him. So, when the orthodontist asked my son, "How's your summer going with your brother away?" I practically had to pick up my jaw from the floor when he answered.

"It's just awful. There's nothing to do. No one to play with. I can't wait till he comes back." I couldn't have been more shocked had I been poked with a cattle prod.

Notwithstanding that shock, I consider myself as something of a "gender wonk," having produced three boys and a girl.

Truth to tell, from the triumphant moment when my first labor culminated in a shout of "It's a boy!" it seemed only natural and just that my next child should be a girl. I pined for a girl, whom I could lovingly dress in creme-colored onesies, lavender dresses, and every shade of pink stretchy from pearl to purple. After two more consecutive cries of "It's a boy!" though, my house was filled with miniature masculine attire. There wasn't an NBA, NFL or NHL insignia that wasn't stamped on someone's pajamas, sweater, or underwear. This doesn't include all the trucks, wrenches, and manly animal motifs (pigs, elephants, bison) adorning the rest of my sons' wardrobes.

As the only female in the family now, I had become greatly outnumbered. During my fourth pregnancy, I didn't think much about having a girl any more than I thought about winning the California state lottery. What were my chances anyway? I was still using the same baby order form, and so far, our inventory seemed overstocked with Y-chromosomes. I reminded myself daily that God would only have given me this many sons if He felt I could handle them. I hoped He was right, as I watched my little crew of linebackers and carpenters tear around the house, ripping molding off the wall and unscrewing the pipes beneath the laundry sink.

Toward the end of that pregnancy, I shuttled regularly between the OB's office and the ultrasound center. Now, my husband and I had always agreed not to find out the sex of our children before they were born. (Though, by son number three, no one was surprised.) But as I lay on the examining table at the screening center watching my child on video, the technician asked me if I wanted to know its sex.

"No," I lied.

I was sent back the next week, and the same tech asked me the same question.

I paused briefly and lied again.

By the following week, I feared that my resolve would crumble if she asked me a third time. Why did she torment me this way? Come to think of it, she did have a slightly sinister Eastern European accent.

As I lay on the table, the inevitable occurred. "Do you want to know the sex of the baby?" she teased.

I couldn't stand it anymore. Digging my nails into the

side of the chair, I said through gritted teeth, "It's another boy, isn't it?"

"Nooooo," she replied slyly.

My heart skipped a beat. I dug my nails in, much deeper this time. "Are you SURE?" What if she were wrong? I had heard stories like this, inaccurate readings that transformed labia into testicles, and vice versa. I didn't think I was emotionally stable enough to withstand any gender confusion at this point.

"Yes, I'm VERY sure!" she said, smiling.

Could it be? Was I really going to acquire a female ally in the house? Inexplicably, I felt the urge to have a Victory Manicure.

"Really, REALLY sure?" My nails had now made permanent imprints in the arms of the chair.

"Yes, congratulations!" she said.

I can't say that in my greatly expectant condition I felt "light," but I did feel vindicated by this ultrasound verdict. I felt serene, as though the heavens had smiled upon me. I thought guiltily of my friends who still had only boys or only girls at home.

I asked my husband if he wanted me to share my new intelligence with him. He declined. But this was hardly news I could keep inside, so when the obstetrician finally shouted, "It's a girl!" my husband was the last person in the Western Hemisphere to whom this was a news flash.

It took me about two years to fully absorb the reality of having a daughter. It was kind of like all those months when I kept glancing at my ring finger after my husband had finally proposed, to make sure the diamond was still there. In my gauzy happiness, I succumbed to what my friend called "fem overload." I pierced my daughter's ears when she was only a year old, something I never would have done if she had been my first or even second child. Feeling guilty for her tears at the earring store where I had it done, I, too, began to cry. Just then, a woman from India who happened to be in the store sidled over to me. She looked stern, yet compassionate.

"Don't be upset!" she said in a clipped Indian accent. "You HAD to do this!" She was deadly serious. And I wasn't about to argue with a woman with such an impressive mark in the middle of her forehead.

"I did?" All I thought I had done was violate my husband's express wishes on this subject, but now I learned that I had performed a sacrosanct Eastern cultural custom on my Jewish American daughter.

"Yes, of course!" The woman was adamant. "See? She has stopped crying already. You did the right thing." She patted me on the head and left.

Obviously, the color blue was verboten for my daughter's wardrobe. And I enjoyed flaunting her Royal Pinkness throughout the town. But the difference between daughters and sons transcends lacy socks, Mary Janes, dresses with sashes and pastel hair ribbons.

Most striking was the behavioral difference between her and her brothers. For example, my boys had trained me never, ever to take my eyes off them in public, since they all had a penchant for letting go of my hand and suddenly darting into oncoming traffic. My heart rate had gone on autopilot hyper-acceleration, as I anticipated each of my next sprints to snatch a son from the jaws of danger. I even tried one of those kid leashes, which ceased to look silly and appeared as essential as car seats. But here's the rub: In my experience, any kid feisty enough to need a kid leash is also wily enough to avoid being hooked into it.

When I sauntered about town with my daughter, however, she just stood next to me calmly, with no apparent plans to rocket away. I soon felt foolish, turning my head around constantly, always somehow surprised that she was still there, and rather contentedly at that.

This isn't to say that having three brothers didn't have an impact on her. Once, when she was three years old and playing in her room with a friend from down the block, I came to see how the girls were getting along. They were just beginning an argument over who would be the mommy and who would be the baby. With the argument at an impasse, my daughter took one of her brother's squirt guns, aimed it at her friend, and said, "You be the baby or I'll shoot!"

Despite this lesson in conflict resolution obviously learned from her brothers, however, my daughter has been almost quintessentially feminine. Like nearly every other female on the face of the planet, she has been programmed with software different from that of her brothers. And, while I suppose I knew all about male-female differences before she was born, having a girl has underscored them as indelibly as the black permanent marker she once decided would artistically enhance our Wedgwood-blue leather sectional. So, for all you new moms out there who aren't sure what to expect when you get a boy or girl, I think the contrasts can be pretty much summarized as follows:

Boys like to play games with a high probability of ending up with X-rays and sutures. Specifics of the games vary, of course, but they frequently include pouncing, pummeling, spitting, throwing hard objects at either inanimate or animate objects, jumping out from nowhere to scare other players to death, climbing on rooftops and shouting to pedestrians, leaning out of roller coasters at ninety-degree angles and yelling,

"Hi, Ma!" and sneaking off to the mini-mart for sodas and junk food. This is their idea of fun, so don't try to change it. Just be prepared to start coloring your hair a little earlier than originally planned. If you want to socialize boys to be more tame, and convince them to try to help you make dinner, don't kid yourself that they are going to end up like Wolfgang Puck, devoting their careers to concocting new ways to cook Portobello mushrooms and goat cheese. They're just there for the knives.

When I was a young mother, I refused to buy my boys any toy guns or knives. Like a good student of the 1970s, I wanted to give peace a chance in my house. Ha! What a chump! Although my policy has not changed, and I still cannot bring myself to buy toy weapons, my efforts have been for naught. My boys have created toy guns when they needed them out of whatever materials happen to be around the house: hangers, Legos, tree branches, soda bottles (the one-liter size makes a nifty AK-47), and my grandmother's antique candlesticks. So if you persist in maintaining that you can socialize boys to subsume their naturally occurring, testosterone-driven swashbuckling and not buy them toy guns, go ahead: Make my day.

Girls like to play games that end with a high probability of injured feelings and detailed reenactments of their playmates' most galling insults to their persons. Necessary equipment for girl-play includes hairstyling implements, purses, telephones, high-heeled shoes, nail polish, magazines of alpha males and beautiful women, and their mothers' jewelry boxes. Their games ideally end with marriage, children, and credit cards with generous spending limits. (If you don't believe me, please reference the 45,000 contestants who lined up to qualify as a wife for a far-less-than-perfect stranger on the show

"Who Wants to Marry an Alleged Abusive Barely Qualifying Multimillionaire Who's So Cheap He Reuses Baggies?")

If this depresses you, it shouldn't. Society has always required hunters and gatherers, as well as nesters and fortune hunters. See, our software hasn't changed, just the dimensions of our motherboards.

For you skeptics out there who don't believe me, you are probably not a parent yet. Why not try this experiment to test my theory that males and females are hard-wired completely differently: Say the following list of words to boys and girls. For scientific accuracy, do this with only boys or only girls. You will see that the boys' eyes will light up at what I call the "manly" words, and females will begin to quiver ever so slightly at the "feminine" words.

Words for Manly Boys→	Fem-Overload Words
Astroturf →	Ab crunch
Budweiser →	Bloomingdale's
Competitive spirit →	Commitment
Defensive tackle →	Diffused lights
End zone →	End-of-season clearance
Furlough →	Feelings
Hooters →	Husbands
Megahertz →	Marriage license
Payload →	Perfume
Joystick →	June brides
Fire-Engine Red →	Frosted Mauve
Remote control →	Romance
Sharon Stone →	Tom Cruise
Touchdown! →	Touchup

See? Wasn't that simple? And wasn't I right? Now, scientists try to make this complicated, but it really isn't. If you can accept the fact that even small boys wearing Barney tennis shoes and peanut butter smiles have masculine egos, and like to play to win, your career as a mother won't be any easier. But you will have been fully warned that if you introduce another male into their orbit, such as a brother, they will naturally want to protect their turf.

Just like in the Bible.

Chapter 8

Nature Abhors a Vacuum Cleaner

I just don't get mothers who can keep their homes clean, neat and organized, without a housekeeper on round-the-clock duty. Once my kids are inside the door, they launch an all-out offensive, dive-bombing their backpacks, hurling their shoes toward their next of kin, and advancing toward the den with their reeky socks, just liberated from moist feet.

Yet I want my home to be neat, I really do. So, in my haste to clean up after these pernicious chaos creators, I become a juggler: trying to catch the size sixteen jacket that my son flings toward the couch, swooping low to gather the shoes in their free-fall descent to the hallway floor, and simultaneously inviting a hernia from trying to heft a fifty-pound backpack from the dining room table.

This method of cleanup has the dual distinction of being ineffectual ("Hey, whose brilliant idea was it to put my jacket in HER closet?") AND wimpy. Because invariably, I hear myself call out plaintively, "What do I look like, the maid?" a rhetorical question asked in desperation that invites such knavish responses as, "Nah, she's thinner than you are."

Of course, I know several mothers—without household help—whose homes ARE immaculate, including a sister-in-law who inadvertently laid it on thick when she announced that in her spare time she would become a home organizer. When she visits from out of town, she always scans the premises of my house and offers, "Gee, need any HELP tidying up around here?" Now, I had been taught in classes on religious theology that situations like this should be instructive: Instead of finding the existence of such women an irritant, as I do, I should find inspiration in their example. Rise above your limitations! these classes exhorted me. Become greater than you are! Of course, I never went back to *that* class, and subsequently looked for religious and emotional training on friendlier turf, like the Home Shopping Network.

I was never slovenly, mind you. In my life BC—Before Children—how hard could it have been to find my own bank statements? After all, no small and sticky hands had absconded with them, made a fleet of paper airplanes out of the cancelled checks, and flown them around the house, where they finally crash landed behind a bunk bed. Sure, it's easy to keep your linens folded neatly in the closet when they haven't been morphed into tents over the dining room chairs, or draped over various small people, making them look like miniature Klan members.

Every normal mother must allow her cleanliness and organizational standards to drop exponentially with each additional child, if only for sanity's sake. At least, that's how I cope. I remember once watching a first-time mom snatch a pacifier from the hands of her toddler because—get this—the toddler had let the pacifier drop on a freshly vacuumed carpet! Since it would have been rude to laugh in her face, I had to suddenly excuse myself to the restroom so that I could guffaw out loud.

Here's basically how your litmus test of "clean" evolves as you collect additional children. Let's use the handy, classic example of the toddler dropping a pacifier on the kitchen floor. Consider that the floor doesn't belong to one of these neat-freak kinds of moms, but instead, to a normal mom, like me. Quite frankly, this floor could use a sweep and mop job.

First child: Panic briefly lest the toddler submerge the bacterially compromised pacifier back into his mouth. Then, grab the pacifier and wash with gentle dishwashing detergent. Next, boil a pan of water, immerse cleaned pacifier in boiled water, and send to the Centers for Disease Control to test for microbial residue. Open new pacifier and sterilize with remaining boiled water. Use PACI-Temp temperature gauge to ensure the newly sterilized pacifier is not too hot.

Second child: Pick up pacifier, give it a fast rinse under whatever temperature water flows from the tap, return to toddler.

Third child: Pick up pacifier, swipe on the back of your skirt, and toss back toward toddler.

Fourth or additional child: Say, "Thanks, Agatha, for picking up that dirt clod from the floor with your pacifier. That's a good girl!"

You get the idea. Motherhood is often like a MASH unit or hospital emergency room, where triage is the order of the day. Compared to the fisticuffs flying in the rear bedroom over the disputed ownership of a glow-in-the-dark yo-yo, the idea of a few foreign bacteria entering your baby or toddler's mouth no longer packs the same punch that it once did. This is especially true if the "foreign" bacteria are from a friendly nation with whom we have mutually beneficial trade agreements.

In Los Angeles, where I live, the county grades all restaurants based on the cleanliness of that establishment. The grades are posted prominently in the window of the restaurants, even fancy ones, making them look a little silly. But the law's the law.

You can feel pretty good eating at a place with a grade of "A" or "B." Obviously, you want to avoid grades "C" and below, because they seem to have some sort of vermin infestation that is incompatible with an ambient dining experience.

I'm glad the county hasn't yet decided to invade and grade family kitchens, because, oblivious as children seem to be to mess and dirt, at a certain age they do begin to read. You wouldn't want your child shamed by the following scenario:

"Wanna come over for some Sugar-Smacked Frosted Choco-Cinna-Yum Alphabet cereal?"

"Uh, well, yeah, but why is there an 'F' on your kitchen window?"

"Oh, never mind THAT! We found the roach nest last night. The city people are coming to give us a better grade later today."

"I dunno. Why not come to my house for some spaghetti and ketchup? My mom's kitchen got a 'B.'"

Clearly, we cannot allow the already fragile self-esteem of our tender shoots to shrivel even further due to such humiliating scenes. So let's hope this kind of government intrusion isn't coming our way.

Experienced mothers simply wink at a lot that goes on in the kitchen and behind the den couch, such as the slow decomposition of last season's cherry pits, a few plastic candy wrappers that will never decompose but remain in our nation's landfills until the polar caps melt, and a Popsicle stick with the joke still readable (but probably still not funny). Experienced mothers of multiple children will eventually need to enlist the aid of their older children to help chip away at the piles of laundry, dishes and sweeping.

But when the kids are very young, they often offer, in their innocence and naivete, to pitch in themselves.

For example, when my oldest son was eighteen months old, he toddled over to get the broom and tried to sweep. Since I had a newborn at the time I thought, "Hey, this could be the start of something beautiful!" I gave him the broom and said, "Go for it! God knows I don't want to!" So from that time until he got wise to the fact of his child labor exploitation, (about age three), my eldest son swept the floor. Didn't do a bad job, really.

Making—I mean, encouraging—kids to clean also teaches responsibility. True, the actual cleanliness level may suffer, but your child's self-esteem could skyrocket.

"Is that a smudge on this soup bowl?" an insensitive dinner guest might ask. "Might you happen to have a clean one?"

"No no no!" you reply, maternal protection engines fully engaged. "The bowl is PERFECTLY CLEAN! Bartholomew cleaned it himself! What looks like a smudge to you is really a holographic with his name. Just like with paper bags, where it says 'Inspected by Miranda.' This holographic means the bowl was carefully and expertly washed by Bartholomew!" Of course, this method only works until the kid is about five or six, so enjoy it while it lasts.

Many would-be parents think that babyhood is the messiest time in child rearing, what with little Kyle Tyler flinging his noodles from the high chair to the wall, and little Shelby teepeeing the house with the toilet paper she is unrolling from the bathroom, trailing it behind her like a biodegradable bridal train. As they are in so many areas, these parents are mistaken.

With babies, you can at least contain some messes. Unless they take off their own diapers, for example, you pretty much can be assured that their private business will remain where you want it: private. In the diaper. You have no such assurance, especially with boys, once they are so-called "potty-trained." The phrase "hit or miss" was probably first coined by a mother trying to get her boys to get it in the commode. (Eventually, she probably gave up and encouraged her boys to grow up to be fire fighters, when they could direct their hoses with impunity.)

So bathroom messes are a clear and present danger for many years past diaperhood. Here's another great tip, especially if you have created male children: Never put a toilet-hugging little rug on the floor of your bathroom, even if your mother-in-law brings you one as a housewarming gift. Prepare to clean your bathroom or have it cleaned every hour.

Messes and disorganization can also serve as an effective crime deterrent, especially Legos strewn strategically over the floor. This isn't as preposterous as it sounds. Just imagine that you are a robber targeting a house to break into. Any experienced criminal can pick a lock, but how many can stumble over 4,927 Lego pieces without either tripping or cursing? Even a clay-brained thief will realize that he cannot conduct business as usual with a sprained ankle. Therefore, he will beat a hasty retreat from any home that is Lego-protected.

In my experience, girls have a higher cleanliness consciousness than boys. Many grown women have noticed the same phenomenon. Girls seem to want to be clean, whereas boys often view soap as an instrument of torture that should be banned by Amnesty International. When I ask my daughter if she wants a bath, she's already turned on the water and dumped half a bottle of soap inside before I finish the question. She would stay in there until her next birthday, just lathering and soaking, unless I hauled her out, shriveled like a giant raisin. My boys also need to be hauled—INTO the shower or tub. They enjoy the prospect of getting clean as much as they enjoy the idea of getting their tetanus shots updated.

"Why should I take a bath?" asked my son, the one who skipped past that delicious stage where most kids enjoy helping to clean up. "I'm just going to get DIRTY AGAIN!"

To which I answered: "Why eat? You're just going to get HUNGRY AGAIN! Why sleep? You're just going to get TIRED AGAIN!"

You would think that my irrefutable logic might have swayed him into thinking, "Gee, she's right. I ought to get cracking in that shower, right now!" But it didn't. Boys don't even care when they are emitting powerful and embarrassing body stench, or that they are so packed with grime that they look as if they have just emerged from a coal mine. This is one reason why I bought a microscope. I wish its purpose were to help my children explore the marvels of the universe around them, to take leaves from the ground and examine their beauty and intricacy magnified many times over. But no, I bought this microscope for one reason and one reason only: to prove to my male children that if their own rank odor did not compel them to bathe, if the dirt that had settled like an eighth layer of skin on their bodies did make soap and a washcloth seem like a fine idea, then I would subject their skin to the unforgiving magnification of this microscope to prove that they were harboring millions of marauding microorganisms that needed to be scrubbed off.

One of the most frightening sights I ever saw was when one of my sons had returned from a weeklong visit to friends who lived out of town. I had carefully packed his clothing, with plenty of clean underwear and socks. I instructed him to use the laundry bag I provided for his dirty clothes, which I would wash upon his return. When I opened his suitcase, his laundry bag had a lonely pair of mud-caked jeans and a few shirts with spaghetti sauce on them. But the underwear, every last pair, was still clean.

No, they won't really get it, this business about being clean, until they are interested in girls.

At which point you will pine for the days when they were happy to be dirty all the time.

Chapter 9

"Say Again?" Life As an Older Parent

I was sipping my diet soda, minding my own business, when I spied a casual acquaintance over at the next table. We were both held hostage at one of those giant indoor romp-arenas, where you can take your kids to blow off steam for a couple of hours on cold, rainy days or vacation days from school. This is a primary color PVC wonderland, where kids climb up ladders, crawl through tunnels, slide down chutes and dive into rainbow seas of plastic balls.

Anyway, my curiosity was piqued when I saw Helen. Always bean-thin, Helen was wearing a blouse of a suspiciously generous cut. Now, this woman had already earned my admiration for having her only son at forty-four, and motherhood agreed with her completely. But her son was now seven, which meant that if Helen was in the family way again now, that would make her, well...older.

After we spotted each other, Helen joined me at my table,

and we chatted casually, as I worked very hard to keep my eyes off her tented tum-tum. Fortunately, she put me out of my misery quickly.

"Yep, I'm having another baby!" she announced with a wide grin, and I feigned my happy surprise. As I congratulated her, the questions began to swirl in my mind like a frozen yogurt blend: Which would arrive first? Her new baby or her AARP card? Would baby be graduating from diapers as Helen went into them? Would the government direct-deposit her Social Security checks into her child's college tuition fund?

I wanted to ask Helen how she felt, but before I could say anything, I heard my daughter shriek, "MOMMY! YOU'RE NOT WATCHING ME!"

"Yes, I am watching you!" I said, telling what we mothers might call a harmless white lie. This is not to be confused with even the minutest kind of prevarication that our children might tell us. We've got to teach them right from wrong, after all.

"What did I just do?" my daughter grilled me from the platform leading to an orange slide.

"You just...climbed down the rope?"

"Right!" She seemed pleased, but no more than I was for having guessed right.

"Was I good, Mommy?"

"Fantastic! You were wonderful! It was an Olympic-qualifying climb!"

I then turned back to Helen. "How do you feel?" I asked her, genuinely concerned. Just knowing that she was pregnant at her age made me feel slightly queasy. I knew *I* could never do it.

"Great! Just great!" she answered, and her healthy complexion and eager smile convinced me. Few, if any women, could pull off this kind of trick with Helen's grace and elan.

"MOMMY! COME DOWN THE CHUTE WITH ME!" Helen's son, Jared, shouted to her from the play area. We could see only his head and shoulders, since the rest of his body was submerged in the sea of plastic balls.

"Sure thing, honey!" Helen called. "I'll be back," she said to me with a wink, then whisked herself off to join her son for some gymnastic gyrations.

I was awed. Helen was of an age when most of her friends were popping estrogen tablets, and here she was, nibbling soda crackers and getting her glucose tested. Not only that, she was about to whiz down a huge green chute with her son, not even worrying about her delicate condition.

One of my kids had already tried this gambit with me, urging to get me to go down the chute with him, but I declined. Unlike Helen, I feared that the force of gravity might conspire against me, and that my other kids would have to give me a solid shove from behind in order for me to gain any momentum.

Apparently, Helen's got a lot of company in this new realm of geriatric gestation. News reports of women even older than Helen doing kegel exercises and reading books on Lamaze (albeit with bifocals) are no longer rare. We haven't seen this many births to overripe women since the days of the Bible. In fact, not long before meeting Helen that day, I had read of a 55-year-old woman giving birth to quadruplets, and if I'm not mistaken, a 63-year-old woman produced a new heir, with help from fertility specialists. But according to news reports I read, the 63-year-old had cheated, and her doctor had been plenty mad later on. It appears his upper age limit for in-vitro procedures was fifty-five, and she had lied about her age. Who knew? She didn't look a day over fifty-four.

In a few minutes, Helen returned, looking solidly refreshed from her travels down the chute.

"Sorry I was so long," she apologized. "Jared wanted me to keep going up that ladder with him. But after the fifth time, I told him I needed a break."

I smiled weakly. What a woman!

Although finding myself with a brand new baby and a standing appointment at the hairdressers for a tint job wasn't my idea of ideal planning, I could see that Helen was well equipped to handle it.

"You know, I'm so grateful that today, age is really just a state of mind," said Helen, apparently reading *my* mind and shaming me in the process. "I mean, I don't feel any older now than I did twenty years ago, do you?"

What could I say? I actually did feel older—a lot older—than I had twenty years before. Of course, twenty years ago I wasn't even old enough to buy a bottle of wine, and was still bumbling through what I now call my "youthful indiscretion" phase. But back then, Helen was already well ensconced in a successful career.

"I admire you, Helen," I said. "I don't think I could have another one at...I mean if I was..." Too late. My faux pas had me flummoxed.

"That's okay, I know what you were going to say," she laughed. "You were going to say, 'I don't think I could have another one at your age.' Really, I'm proud to be a trailblazer."

Helen and I had only a few more minutes of conversation because Jared summoned her back for another round of chutes and ladders. Meanwhile, sitting at the table, I contemplated the many social benefits to this budding senior baby boom.

For starters, the marketers would have a field day. Imagine the booming sales of combination wheelchair-joggers!

Supermarket aisles would also be rearranged to make shopping simpler for the older mom or dad. Why not place the Huggies diapers next to the incontinence aids? Flintstones vitamins shrink-wrapped along with each bottle of Geritol? Johnson's baby shampoo next to the Rogaine? Beech-Nut, which already has its line of baby food for Stages 1-4, would add a low-sodium, low-sugar Stage 80-93 line of foods as well. It wouldn't be long before Little Tikes products would be advertised in the pages of *Modern Maturity*. When Golden Books would develop a line of large-type story books. When Disney children's videos would be closed-captioned.

Certainly the older parents would benefit economically. Admissions to movies and museums would be cheaper, since everyone in the family can enjoy either the children's rate or senior discount. And let's not forget the psychological benefits. Older moms, like Helen, would undoubtedly sympathize with baby's developmental stages in a way that younger parents simply could not. For example, an older dad whose own choppers are soaking overnight in a glass may cry along with baby as he rubs the teething gel on the infant's sore gums. A teen anguishing over the heartbreak of acne can commiserate with Mom, who is busy rubbing Porcelana over her liver spots.

There are even linguistic benefits. When one kid asks another, "Did you ask your old man if you can sleep over tonight?" it won't just be a figure of speech. And when the sixth-grade teacher assigns a report in class to research a historical figure, Junior can just wheel Dad right into class to reminisce about his landing at Normandy. These seasoned citizen parents will also neatly eclipse that nagging problem of the generation gap by skipping it altogether.

Of course, all may not be smooth in this picture. Practical considerations will arise. When Mom plays "Ring Around the

Rosy" with her in-vitro-induced triplets, who will help Mom up from the floor when they all fall down? Who will take the kiddies on those amusement park rides that preclude people with heart conditions?

And when the kids become teens, Dad may want to count his Viagra tablets each Saturday night to make sure Sonny hasn't pocketed them for some extra fun. Older parents may also want to stay on the kids' good side in case they need their help in opening those child-proof containers of medicine, which can be so hard on arthritic hands.

But I don't mean to drape a wet diaper over this cheery trend. Minds cleverer than mine are already devising ways to tackle these thorny issues. Meanwhile, this is a trend that seems here to stay. I recently received one invitation to a combination baby shower/retirement party for another dowager I know. I decided to go with a tubby-time theme. I bought a bathtub safety bar for her and a plastic elephant spout cover for the kid.

But for Helen? I'd have to be a lot more creative in the gift-giving department. Watching her cavort with her son, I imagined that soon after the delivery, she'd likely be teaching a combination post-natal/post-menopausal aerobics class over at the YMCA.

With her energy, I suppose the best shower gift would be a year's pass to this indoor children's gym. After all, Helen's kids would need to stay in tip-top shape to keep up with her.

Chapter 10

March of the Miniature Maccabees

A s the holiday season crept up on me again this year, I decided to ask the kids what they wanted for Chanukah. As usual, they applied their creativity to this endeavor in ways that surprised me.

My oldest child requested a $200 electronic gizmo, and a few $40 games to go with it. This did not surprise me.

My second-born then gave me his list. "I want a color Game Boy. I'd also like to go to Disney World. And, what I want most is for you to get a prescription."

"A prescription?" I asked. "Do you mean a subscription? For a magazine?"

"No, Mom, a prescription."

"For whom? For what?" I wondered.

"For my brother, that's who! I want him medicated for the rest of the winter. Then maybe I'll have some peace and quiet around here."

My youngest son wanted a dinosaur. A real one. To keep in the bathroom. You know, instead of that silly old plastic elephant in the tub. Barring that, he wanted an alligator. He found my reasons for failing to satisfy his wishes completely unsatisfactory.

My daughter wanted Supreme Court Justice Barbie and to give away her brothers to a poor childless couple.

I found that even though I could not comply with everything on my kids' wish list (though the prescription, multiplied by four, sounded mighty tempting), the Internet became a fast friend. Because if there's one thing I really hate, it's those annual trips to Toys 'R Us, lingering in the aisles trying to decide between a 700-piece construction set and a motorized race car. Each gift selection clearly comes with its own set of risks. For example, any building set has pieces. Lots of lots of pieces. Now, in my experience, sets with pieces (other than flatware and china) tend to be subject to the laws of entropy. Motorized cars will either be raced around the house, bashing into your walls and chipping the paint, or will end up lost in a neighbor's shrubbery. Any gift carries the risk of being compared to a sibling's gift as inferior, more educational, or in some other way less desirable.

Though China may be one of the only nations on Earth that has not at some point in history persecuted the Jewish people, the words "Made in China" stamped upon a toy are nonetheless enemies of Chanukah happiness, toy-wise. I once watched a "Made in China" toy self-destruct after oh, I'd say, about forty-two seconds, giving a very literal meaning to the term "immediate gratification." The political converse is also true:

German-made items will last until your children have great-grandchildren of their own. Still, this opens up lots of quality hand-me-down opportunities.

Ironically, when my children were very young, the amount of time I spent deliberating over their gifts was in inverse proportion to the amount of enjoyment they derived from them. However, one thing was always certain: They would absolutely flip for the box it came in.

I could never bring myself to do what I was tempted to do, and just give them a festively wrapped, empty box, to see if they would notice that there was nothing inside. Because for several years, these boxes proved far more durable and had longer-lasting entertainment value than the gifts that had been diligently wrapped inside. These boxes morphed into forts, makeshift furniture, miniature tunnels and secret hideouts, while the expensive set of blocks and electronic cash register they had housed had been ditched weeks before.

I am not so heartless as to give a completely recyclable gift, so I ended up languishing in indecision at the toy emporium instead. That was then. Now that we live in a dotcom world, I can languish in indecision without even leaving the house, as I click my way to holiday cheer at my computer screen. This year, I thought I got a pretty good deal. A half-dozen cyber-toy emporia dangled enticing offers of free gifts and coupons as a means of snagging my Visa number. To qualify for my discount, all I had to do was type in the special, just-for-me, Judy Gruen, secret code along with my order to get ten bucks whacked off my total. Only trouble was, the code was so long that even had I been a minimum wage-worker, it might not have been worth my time to try to type in a formula like this:

ONLEN9=8987012ID0TWD6666446546SPNDS0000002 90MCHC830TIMDONGTHSBBPLU60895497UMSTBEEECRZY. Of course, accidentally striking a single wrong key would invalidate the coupon, and you would need to begin tapping in the code all over again.

Now, once I zapped my order in, the cyber store would instantaneously send me another coupon code, good for another ten bucks off my next order, provided the order was placed before the milk in my refrigerator began to smell funny. It took all my sale-loving powers to resist this lure. I had to forcibly desist from thinking of all the birthday parties for which I would have gifts at the ready if I only heeded this e-commerce call.

But shockingly, the Chanukah miracle I experienced this year was neither that my latkes didn't weigh more than the local phone directory, nor that the kids didn't accidentally set the couch on fire through their exuberant candle-lighting, but that I managed not to shop online for eight continuous days.

I also tried to infuse some religious import to our holiday. Before I let the kids rip into their presents, I meant to test them. I wanted to see if they still knew more about Chanukah than they did about Kwanzaa, or Casimir Pulaski Day. I secretly hoped that they could recall at least something of the miraculous victory of their ancestors, biblical scholars untrained in the ways of war, over the mighty Syrian-Greeks.

"Okay now, who remembers the name of the leader of the Maccabees?" I asked four sets of eyes that were super-glued to a pile of gifts in dreidel-festooned wrapping paper.

"Charlton Heston!" answered one son, eyes still focused on the gifts, memories of watching *The Ten Commandments* dancing in his head.

"Can we open our presents yet?" asked our daughter.

"Just a minute! This is a religious holiday, not a materialistic bacchanal!" I countered, now regretting that last, teensy toy order. "Just tell me what the miracle of Chanukah was and you can open your gifts!"

For a moment, the kids looked stumped. Then, my eldest offered, "That Steven Spielberg hasn't made it into a movie yet?"

"That you didn't forget to come to my Chanukah performance at school today?" queried another son.

"Oh brother," my husband said. He began to load his arms with the presents and threatened to give them all to the needy.

"We're needy!" pleaded our youngest boy. "We haven't had any Chanukah presents since last year!"

"I know what the Chanukah miracle was," announced my daughter in a confident tone.

"Yes?" my husband and I both said eagerly, yearning to put our family out of its collective misery.

"The Chanukah miracle was that....was that...the oil lasted long enough to make latkes for the whole Maccabee army!"

"Close enough!" I said, stepping aside from the onslaught of four Maccabee descendents heading for their loot. Watching them, I realized that in fact they did have much in common with their great and heroic forebears. Each was willing to fight for what they perceived to be their God-given right. The Maccabees, fighting for freedom of religious expression; our children, attacking with equal zealotry for their share of a material bonanza thinly disguised as religious ritual. The Maccabees, fighting to the death for their spiritual integrity; our children, fighting to the death for the right to be the first to play the new computer game "Galactic Theme Park Implosion."

However, once we'd allowed the kids to explore their booty, my husband and I were able to sit back and bask in the glow of our small, flickering Chanukah lights and the sounds of happy children at play. Best of all, the Environmental Protection Agency made no move to declare my homemade, oil-slicked latkes an ecological disaster. From where we sat, too full to move, there was peace on Earth, and good will toward siblings.

Chapter 11

Why Guar Gum Is Really a Vegetable

I suppose I shouldn't brag that my four children really eat a balanced diet. One eats protein, another eats vegetables, one drinks milk, and all eat foods that begin with consonants. Especially the letter P.

P is a favorite food letter in our house, because many of the kids' most-loved foods begin with it, specifically, pizza, popcorn, peanut butter, pop (as in soda), and potatoes (as in French-fried).

I've done all kinds of crazy things to get my kids to eat vegetables, especially when their behavior was another P word: picky. We had reached the point where the only green food they would eat were bananas that looked like they had been shipped from Central America about two weeks early. But when their palates became simply too discriminating to bear, I realized I had to do something. Now, "discriminating" used to be a compliment, at least when it came to tastes in food and wine. But I realized my kids' discrimination had gotten completely out of control when they refused to eat foods based on color as well as national origin. Clearly, this was very un-American and intolerant of them. The only color they seemed to always like, though, was an eerie neon blue, generally only found in Popsicles that appear to have been concocted at NASA. So, like all moms, I had to perform feats of mental gymnastics, thinking up new and insidious ways to get my children to eat foods other than just those of the eerie neon blue variety.

One of my best ideas, I thought, was the alphabet menu phase.

"Guess what, everyone? Tonight we're only eating foods that start with the letter A. Won't that be fun?"

The preschool-aged kids were happy as puppies. One even got so excited that he nearly did something else puppy-like on the floor. I watched the older kids begin to ponder the implications of this for them.

"What're we having?" one asked suspiciously.

"Apples, asparagus, arugula salad, and antipasti!" I said proudly.

"Who's arugula?" my daughter asked.

"What's antipasti?" several demanded.

"Must be the opposite of pro-pasti," offered my resident wise guy.

When I told them that the term "antipasti" was an Italian word meaning lots of deli meats with occasional smatterings of cracked pepper, they turned up their noses.

"Wait!" I said, as they began to file out of the kitchen and head toward a friendly neighbor's house. "We're going to have regular salami. That counts as antipasti. Sort of."

At this, they collided over one another to get to the table, now more eager to embark on this new adventure in dining. In keeping with the theme of the day, I promised them a dessert made almost entirely of artificial flavorings if they would only agree to roll an asparagus spear inside a salami slice, thus forcing a vegetable down their throats.

The next night, we had bananas, beef stew with artificial bacon chips on top, and a brussels sprout that I cut into five uneven leafy pieces. We were having fun with this, and I was walking around feeling pretty darned proud of myself for this flash of inspiration. After all, I was teaching my kids nutrition, spelling, and multiculturalism, all at the same time. It was interactive learning at its best. I started feeling less guilty that I never, ever packed my kids lunches with those ridiculous pita pocket sandwiches that many parenting magazines suggest you make to get young Cody to eat. These sandwiches also have themes, by the way, but who on Earth will make Mr. Rogers's face out of cream cheese, two black olives, a raisiny smile and a twist of pimiento? First of all, what kid eats pimiento? But even more important, how do these "faces" not look as if they have been run over by the school bus by the time Cody unearths it from his backpack under twenty-two pounds of books?

But I digress. The C night was also easy, with carrots, cole slaw, chicken, cantaloupe and a hint of carrageenan.

By the time we got to D I sensed I was losing steam. No one liked deviled eggs, or daikon salad, but the dextrose was well received. However, kids cannot live on dextrose alone, so I broke down and drove to the deli, where we had more salami. I ended the evening with a daiquiri.

We plodded on through the next few letters, but, like an old record player stuck repeating a single chord, we stayed on H for a solid week, since that meant hot dogs, Heinz ketchup, hydrolized vegetable protein and, my children insisted, Halloween candy. And we don't even *do* Halloween.

Meanwhile, we haven't managed to move past P, for the reasons stated above. Besides, the end of the alphabet was definitely presenting problems. What, for example, would I do about Q night? Go quail hunting? And what about R? Could I really serve them radishes, red dye number 40, and a red herring? But, sensing my desperation, the kids goaded me on. They challenged me to serve an "X-rated" dinner, a challenge that I accepted by placing a chest X-ray on the table.

"If you don't start eating what I put on the table, this is all that will be left of you," I warned in my sternest voice.

Ready to give up, I combined Y and Z nights together, and all I can tell you is that there are more foods than you realize on supermarket shelves that contain yellow dye number 6 and zinc. However, I don't recommend yogurt-yam soufflé, as the soufflé tends to fall precipitously as you carry it from the oven to the table. The soufflé doesn't fall on its own so much as it senses the despair of its audience, and crumples in defeat. Fortunately, I had Alpha-Bit cereal waiting in the wings as a backup.

After we finished counting our ABCs for dinner, I decided I would just be grateful for anything they were willing to eat that wasn't eerie neon blue. Anyway, none of my kinds are as picky as the 10-year-old boy I knew who would only eat hot dogs and spaghetti. Not mostacelli. Not macaroni. Not vermicelli. Not linguini. Not rotini. Not even spaghettini. Just spaghetti. And no sauce. But his mother, if I am not mistaken, only ate brown rice and plain yogurt, so the way I figure, she had it coming.

I bet I'm not the only woman whose eating habits changed for the worse after kids came along. When my oldest child first graduated from pureed mush to "regular" food, I began finishing his leftover scrambled eggs, peas, and bits of kiwi off his highchair tray, simply because I hated to see perfectly good food go to waste. It dawned on me only later that it had been four months since I had actually chewed anything solid. Furthermore, harsh as this reality is, even micro bits of cold, bland baby leftovers have calories. It was tough, but I managed to wean myself off Junior's culinary castoffs. I also began giving him smaller portions. This wasn't as easy as you might think. As a Jewish mother who is genetically programmed to cook and serve for sixteen people even if it's just my husband and me for breakfast, the retraining took several months, including eight sessions of past-life regression therapy.

My short-lived alphabet menu phase aside, I have made many terminally stupid blunders when feeding my kids. The worst one has been falling into the trap of making two dinners each night. I'd make a kid-friendly dinner, with various shaped noodles playing the starring role and vegetables in a cameo appearance. Then I'd prepare an adult dinner, featuring foods demanding an acquired taste, such as salmon croquettes, baked potatoes, and trendy salad greens so bitter that only upscale restaurants can get away with charging $8 for a little plate full of them.

Many writers who wax eloquent and romantic about families often say that "food is love." They are right, sometimes. Children will equate food with love if all you feed them are those sticky fruit roll-ups that stain their teeth and mouth so badly that you need turpentine to get the color off. The truth is that most of the time with kids, food isn't love—it's war! After all, a person can stand to make only so many "happy face" dinners out of bananas (the mouth and eyes), raisins (eyeballs), chocolate chips (eyebrows), thin carrot circle (nose), and plain spaghetti (hair). At some point, a mom has to get on with her life and get down to the business of forcing nutrition into the small people who will one day produce her grandchildren.

"Whatever's on the table is what there is to eat," is my battle cry during these food skirmishes, as the kids look with horror at a spinach quiche I have placed in front of them. (The instant solidarity among the children at times like this is touching, however.) I try not to think about the fact that I gave them no warning about suddenly changing the rules. "If you don't like it, there's always breakfast tomorrow," I add, suddenly reminding myself of many nasty child-hating Dickensian characters. I don't worry that they'll actually go hungry. The oldest two kids always keep a stash of candy bars under their beds for emergencies just like these. And the youngest, too fearful of an empty tummy, will grimace but swallow enough to ward off famine until the next morning.

Another dumb thing I have done is to make the patently absurd statement, "I am not a waitress!" in response to their forty-seven simultaneous requests for apple juice, orange juice, ketchup, soy sauce, sliced cheese and other accompaniments to their repasts.

"Yeah, Mommy's not a waitress," one will chime in, rallying to my defense.

"Yeah, get it yourself!" another will pile on, now seizing the serendipitous opportunity to help shame a sibling.

But as I made the statement, I was removing another dish from the oven, pouring somebody something liquid in a plastic cup, and retrieving additional napkins and cutlery. I realized then that I wasn't only a waitress: I was also chief cook and bottle washer. Anyway, when was the last time you had a waitress who cut your meat for you?

I think I now know why the concept of the family dinner has become such a hallowed institution. In fact, "experts" (whoever they are) have proclaimed that one of the strongest predictors of future success in life is having grown up in a family that preserved this tradition. And no wonder. Between all the bickering and accusations flying faster than the ketchup out of the bottle and onto a kid's shirt, trying to eat dinner under the stress of constant fighting can give anyone a skin thick enough to withstand whatever onslaughts the world will dole out in later years. Having dinner with members of the same family clan is like a nightly hazing ritual—only the strongest survive. After years in the proving ground of the kitchen table, nothing can stand in the way of future success.

"What? You say this department eats its new managers alive? Ha! You say that colleagues are quick to criticize and find fault with others' work? Ha! Ha! That's NOTHING! I grew up in a home where the whole family had dinner together every night! There isn't an insult I haven't already heard that I can't 'digest,' if you know what I mean. Those family dinners helped me become the forthright, confident person I am today. You couldn't have picked a more qualified candidate for this job, sir!"

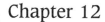

Chapter 12

Culture Mulcher Mom

One day, just as my oldest son was learning to read, we drove by a billboard that caught his attention. "Hey, Mommy! It says, 'Get your butt in here!'" He and his brother laughed, looking at the advertisement from a large clothing retailer. They relished this linguistic opportunity; they couldn't have gotten away with speaking like that at home.

"Hmm," I said, "guess no one remembered to teach them about proper language!"

As we drove on, I began to feel almost as unzipped as the girl who had exposed her lower abdomen to the masses on that billboard. So long, innocence! I thought. Now that he could read, I couldn't stop my son from imbibing lessons in Vulgarity 101: Marketing in America. The minute we got home, I looked up the corporate office of the clothing retailer and called.

"Hello there," I greeted the marketing manager when he

came on the line. "I saw your billboard today in my neighborhood. Near nudity, sophomoric language. Really high concept. I don't know how much you paid for it, but you've just lost my business permanently. And with four kids, I have lots of derrieres to cover."

I waited for his response, hoping he would defend his company's position, since I was in the mood for a verbal demolition derby. I had always regretted skipping forensics in college.

"Yes, we realize this campaign may have been a mistake," he replied. "We're canceling it and coming up with something new that we believe will be better received. We hope you'll give us another chance."

"I'm glad you recognize the mistake," I said, a little disappointed that it had been so easy. I commended him and the company for acting quickly, but still essayed my opinion on the matter in a letter to the president of the company.

I needn't have worried about it being "too easy" to moonlight as Culture Mulcher Mom. First of all, in the past several years, our society has become coarser than kosher salt. Do we really need to hear radio advertisements, while we are driving around enjoying a cup of coffee, for a new weight-loss compound that might cause "urgent and embarrassing gastrointestinal distress, accompanied by a subsequent narrowing of social circles?" Am I enriched in any way by knowing about a former elder statesman's erectile dysfunction?

During my little campaign against philistinism, I've called television and radio broadcasters, billboard companies and other businesses to register my protest at their kitschy and crass programs, products and slogans. One of my targets was an abominable billboard featuring a near-nude with mammaries the size of grain silos. Apparently, the model's great fun in life was plying her garish, liposucted body on billboards throughout my fair city. I called the billboard company that had rented her the space, and made sure to do it when my kids were listening.

"Haven't you ever heard of something called the First Amendment?" the company rep challenged me.

"Sounds familiar. Haven't you ever heard of something called 'taste'?"

"Well, times have changed. Besides, you're the only one who's complained."

However, I persisted, and can count among my greatest civic achievements the deconstruction of at least four such billboards. Somehow, the mayor forgot to give me the key to the city for my efforts.

This line about my being "the only one" to complain became a familiar refrain. Well, if they were trying to make me feel like a kook, as if I had suddenly begun claiming Elvis sightings, it wouldn't wash with me. I had kids to protect! I was on a mission!

The phone became my trusted ally in this campaign. After accidentally hearing a small yet repugnant snippet from a radio show, I called the station. They recognized my voice, or was it my ring?

"You again?" the woman said. "Why don't you just save yourself some time and enter our number on your 'speed dial?' What's bugging you today?"

I told her.

"Well, you're the only one who complained about our interview. Rapper WD-40 is the hottest new musical artist around. Sorry we missed some of his four-letter words before we could bleep them out, but what the hell. It's nothing people haven't heard before."

"That may be because our society has suffered the cultural equivalent of Chinese water torture. You've been raining droplets of vulgarity on us so long that most people have forgotten what it's like not to feel offended."

This standpat position is a hard sell when I'm speaking to people too young to remember a time when "edgy" was a criticism and "judgmental" could be construed as something positive. They are clearly bored by having to listen to an old mossback like me.

But I soldier on, undeterred. Because sometimes I get results. And even when I don't, I like to challenge the brain matter ostensibly hidden behind that sea of forehead piercings.

After taking my kids bowling on one occasion, I decided it was time to score a strike against the chain that owned the alley. We had managed to bowl two games, with a whopping average score of eighty-nine. The kids triumphantly kicked off their bowling shoes and headed over to the video arcade. I paid as quickly as possible and skedaddled over to the arcade to steer them away from the most violent games. Most had names like "Happy Hit Men's Conquest" and "Megamurder Match-Up," and I noted that there were ratings slapped on each machine. These ratings ranged from "Fun for the Whole Family" (one game) all the way to "Gives The Gambini Brothers the Shivers" (twelve games).

This time, I wrote a letter.

While your alleys try to appeal to families and camp groups, I wrote to the vice-president of the company, *your endorsement of games whose sole aim is execution or terrorism seems to me somehow incongruous. Of course, I could be wrong.*

A few days after sending my missive, the vice-president

called me.

"I'll have you know that we've already removed the most violent games from all our alleys," he said proudly.

"Really? That's remarkable," I said. "Tell me, what could be more violent than 'Frenzied Felons on Furlough'? Those mutilation graphics and screaming sound effects are bone-chilling."

"Well, you'd be surprised, but there are far worse than that. For example. . ."

"NO!" I stopped him. "I most definitely do not want to know what those are." I still hadn't recovered from a screening of the thriller *Jagged Edge* fifteen years earlier. I certainly didn't need this guy feeding me more potent nightmare material.

"Okay, fine. Anyway, even though we have already cleaned up the really bad games, I'm still going to share your letter with the board of directors at our next meeting," he said. "The problem is, our patrons ask for these games. We're just responding to market forces."

"Hey, with my credit limit, I should be construed as a market force. Also, next time you visit one of your alleys, please note the glassy look in the eyes of your trigger-happy young 'patrons,'" I said. "Frankly, I don't think either of us would want to accidentally take their parking space after they finished ten or twenty rounds of 'Bestial Bob Slays the Mob.'"

"You have a point there. Anyway, no offense, but you Americans are a little puritanical. You don't know how good you have it in terms of media violence. I'm from Australia, and lemme tell you, on Aussie TV, anything goes!"

I decided to take his word for it and made a mental note to cross off the land Down Under from our list of vacation spots.

My kids have come to expect my activism. Perhaps they find security in knowing that they are not the sole subjects of my quest for taste and manners. I'm also an equal opportunity crusader, and don't limit my aim to billboards and bowling alleys. Once, on the way to my car from a store, we passed a young man carrying on a cell phone conversation replete with expletives. My son stole a glance at me, wondering if I would respond. I tried to size up the young man, wondering if he could be dangerous. After all, I have a job to do, and I need to be well above room temperature to be able to do it. But I determined that he was probably harmless, so I said, "Hey, watch your language!"

The man looked stunned. Who was this cultural crusader getting on his case? My son and I proceeded to our car, leaving the conversational pollution monger hanging mid-curse.

I mean, isn't it enough that I've got to police my own kids? Why is it also necessary to say things such as, "Pardon me, but would you mind changing this station from heavy metal to something a little lighter? After all, this is a kid's hair salon." Or, "Hey there, would you mind moving these magazines to a more discreet section of the supermarket? I came here for laundry detergent, eggs and milk, not because I felt like explaining to my kids what 'homo-eroticism' is."

Mind you, these are the *consumer* magazines aimed at women, not those cheesy skin mags that men look at while standing behind a curtain at a newsstand.

I can't stop my kids from reading, but I still try to censor where I can. I often put the entertainment section of the newspaper in the recycling bin before they can see it. Who needs kids reading TV listings like this one: "Little Archie asks his parents Kit and Tyne if they will marry. Meanwhile, Kit discovers condoms in Tyne's purse that aren't his brand."

And forget about trying to catch the news with kids around:

"Mom, who's the president having sex with now?" the young children of one of my friends asked her after gleaning a newspaper headline. Teaching the facts of life wasn't supposed to be this way. But the president did say he put a top priority on education. I guess I didn't realize the kind of education he had in mind.

A parent has to be quick on the draw to interrupt other news flashes like these:

"...and the county coroner said that he had found half of a Cobb salad in the deceased's stomach, putting the time of death at about 10:45...."

"...fired twenty-seven rounds before turning the weapon on himself..."

"Oscar-winning actress Amanda Sheath confirmed to the press through her spokeswoman that she is pregnant by Calvin Suave, whom she met while on location in Borneo last fall. Sheath denied previous reports that she would 'commit suicide' if she gains more than eight pounds during the pregnancy. The couple has no plans to marry."

Isn't it ironic? Smokers have to huddle in the cold because second-hand smoke is bad for the rest of us. So why is second-hand cultural pollution more healthful?

Meanwhile, I drive along, ever alert for my next opportunity for a little "landscape architecture," and I keep my cell phone near by, ready to do battle again.

It's a dirty job, but somebody's got to do it.

Chapter 13

The "Me-Too" Tabernacle Choir

I am sitting in the waiting room of my pediatrician's office—again. If possession is nine-tenths of the law, I must own half this waiting room, along with examination rooms 3 (Winnie the Pooh motif), 4 (horses and carousels) and 5 (something related to astrophysics, if I'm not mistaken). I think I'm about halfway toward earning my own designated parking spot in the back.

Actually, I should count my blessings, because my kids have suffered only the garden-variety childhood maladies. But multiply your sinus infections, rashes, impetigo, ear infections, flu, ringworm, chicken pox, and backyard lacerations by four, and you can rack up a lot of frequent-patient mileage shuttling back and forth between home and the doc's office. Once, in perhaps our strangest medical emergency, one of my sons—on a dare from a classmate—took a plastic teddy bear eye from arts and crafts class and jammed it into his ear. This necessitated a quick run to the pediatrician, who could not pry it out and who immediately sent us to an ear, nose, throat and plastic teddy bear eye specialist, who gingerly removed it. At least that was one time when I could credibly claim to my son that he must have had eyes in the back of his head.

When a new clerk at the pharmacy asks me if I've ever had a prescription filled there before, it takes me a while to stop laughing and answer the question. Usually, she gets the idea.

Sure, we worry when our kids are sick. It pains us to see them in true distress, and we suddenly miss the normally boisterous behavior that loudly proclaims their robust health. But honestly, sometimes it's hard to tell if kids are really ill or just faking. Mine are each so eager to display symptoms, and the rest so quick to try and piggyback on a perceived opportunity to stay home and watch videos, I've needed to hone my powers of perception and diagnosis.

Just recently, my daughter ran into my room in the early morning and started jumping up and down on my bed. "I'm sick just like my brothers!" she said in between jumps. "I've got a sore throat and a cold!" Jump, bounce, bounce, jump. "I should stay home too!" she said mid-summersault.

"Look, Ma, I've got this cut," says another, joining the "Me-Too" Tabernacle Choir. He hikes up his pants leg to show me something requiring X-ray vision to see.

"Where?" I ask, leaning in close but seeing only the requisite dirty knee.

"It was there yesterday at lunchtime! It really was! It was gushing blood—(anything of pinkish to red appearance on the skin, usually the size of an atomic particle or smaller)—and I even went to the nurse's office!"

Now, the "Me-Too" Tabernacle will not be deterred even

after you have dusted off the family microscope to search for evidence of this "gushing" blood, and failed to find any.

"Yeah, Mommy, I have all these scratches that itch!"

"Perhaps it's time to reintroduce yourself to the shower. That itching just might resolve itself."

"Oh no, I don't think so," the child protests, and before you know it, the assembled masses are stripping to their skivvies in the family room to reveal the most fantastic complaints known to medicine: "bumps" somewhere below the fourth or fifth layer of epidermis; a pain in the knee that flares up only upon swallowing broccoli; aches in the left heel; and vague stomach upsets that only increase their appetites. These symptoms are invisible to the naked eye, and subsequent visits to our licensed, board-certified physician cannot reveal their cause or authenticity. They can erupt at any time, but are most likely to present themselves when the kids see you after school or think about you as they pass the nurse's office on the way to math class. Ear infections, as we all know, will erupt forty-eight hours before the family is scheduled to get on an airplane.

Once, I let my son stay home for a suspicious complaint of fatigue and headache. I left him with the housekeeper while I ran errands. About an hour later, I called him to check in.

"How are you doing, sweetie?" I asked.

"Not so good," he said, his voice weak, though my Mother Radar suspected the tone was practiced. "I feel really dizzy."

"Dizzy! You've got to get into bed then, right away!"

"No, I don't! I didn't mean 'dizzy,' exactly." Clearly I had interrupted a *Power Ranger* rerun.

"Well, what DID you mean?"

"I was exaggerating," he fessed up. "I don't really need to

lie down...Well, maybe I should on the couch by the TV..."

It got to a point where my kids had worn out the battery on my internal "Bunkum-meter," and I could no longer distinguish between actual physiological symptoms and their medical masquerades. Because, even after they had been proven sick as clinically defined by the National Institutes of Health, they were darned reluctant to ever acknowledge an improvement in their health. Doing so would have meant relinquishing the spot on the den couch where they had left their body imprint for the last week under their germy blanket. So I got tough.

"From now on, NOBODY stays home from school unless he or she's got a fever of 100 degrees or higher and projectile vomiting. If you've got a headache, I'll give you a Tylenol. If your tummy hurts, I'll give you plain toast for breakfast. No more mystery complaints."

This shut them up, at least until bedtime. That is when, as all parents know, the most astonishing quasi-medical or psychological problems arise, all of which, remarkably, will prevent the child from falling asleep! Symptoms appear only after the child has been tucked under the blanket, and just seconds before you are on the verge of a conversation with your spouse for the first time in a week.

Here are some of the complaints often heard in our home:

"My tooth needs to fall out so I can't sleep."

"My hair might stick up tomorrow morning if I go to sleep tonight."

"I don't know what to dream about."

"It says here that my pajamas are 'flame retardant.' Does that mean my pajamas are stupid?"

"I'm too clean from my bath and I'm worried my friends won't recognize me tomorrow."

"I'm itchy all of a sudden."

"My head hurts a lot, especially in my stomach."

"I think I have fever."

"I just remembered a have a book report due tomorrow."

"I think I'm going to throw up." (These last two are often related.)

Biting this bait falls under the category of Stupid Parent Tricks and must be dealt with severely. Sympathy must be withheld, even from small children wearing footie pajamas. In one such case, my friend's son came out of bed to claim, with a most earnest expression, that his "blankie hoit."

Still and all, mothers need to walk that tightrope between warm and fuzzy empathy for our children's aches and pains and keeping our "Bunkum-meters" razor sharp. I must confess, sometime after the plastic teddy bear eye otolaryngology emergency and an unrelated case of "itchy right eyebrow," I became perhaps too tight-fisted in doling out sympathy. I was therefore rewarded, probably by Divine justice, with a slew of children's ailments.

So, when they got ear infections, so did I. (By the way, these really do hurt.) Our antibiotics were lined up in the refrigerator like little pink soldiers; mine in tablet form in the cupboard. And, during one dreadful week when my kids started breaking out with chicken pox one by one, I also waited my turn for the oatmeal bath treatment. I don't know which was more mortifying: trying to care for them when I was also ill, or the sight of myself in the mirror (something I avoided for two weeks afterward). At least so far I have managed to avoid cradle cap, lice, and knocking out any teeth by jumping from the wall in the alley into our neighbor's yard. I think that these other maladies have done the job. Because believe me, when I was down along with them, I really felt their pain.

Now the darned thing is, mothers aren't allowed to get sick. It's not in our contract. When we are ailing, Daddy is on for double-duty, and, try as he might, he cannot manage to prevent certain "sympathetic" visits from children who are eager to have something other than frozen waffles for dinner.

"Mommy? Are you sleeping?" children will ask, even as you lie there with your eyes closed, in a sound yet febrile sleep. It is useless to pretend not to hear them, since if you do, they will likely try to pry your eyelids open with their fingers. So, as you force yourself to open one eye, which feels as heavy as wet sand, you mumble, "I was. Where's Daddy?"

"He's packing lunches for tomorrow. He said I should see if you need anything."

"I need sleep," you say, closing your eye again.

"Mommy? When will you get better? Remember you said we could go to the store and buy a new computer game? Remember? You said it would be tomorrow, and today is tomorrow."

"Yes, honey, but I can't. I'm sick. We'll go when I'm better. Now, if you leave me alone so I can sleep, I might get well faster, and then we might get to the store faster."

Now that you have put it in terms the child can relate to, he or she will beat a hasty retreat, but leave your bedroom door wide open so you can hear loud shouts such as these:

"Come to the table! Daddy says!"

"SHHHHH!!!! Mommy's sleeping!"

"YEAH, MOMMY'S SLEEPING! STOP YELLING!"

"I WASN'T YELLING LOUD! I WAS JUST TELLING YOU THAT DADDY SAID TO BE QUIET! YOU WERE THE ONE WHO WAS YELLING!"

I think, all in all, it's a lot easier for us moms to simply take our vitamins every day. It's just too exhausting to get sick.

Chapter 14

Travel Turbulence

Without meaning to, other mothers often make me feel woefully inadequate. Sometimes it's the moms who bake birthday cakes in the shape of steam engines, complete with button-candy portholes and licorice steam stacks. Sometimes it's the moms who have their entire year's calendar mapped out by late August, with "science project" already on their "To Do" list for the week of April fourth. But the moms whose efficiency and creativity sting me the most are those who can speak blithely about their "family vacations," a phrase that's just as much an oxymoron as "rap music." The very idea that a whole family can strap themselves in happily for a five-hour ride to anywhere and emerge unscathed, both physically and psychologically, is a skill my husband and I have yet to master.

"My kids love being in the car," a former friend once told me, not realizing that every detail she recounted was another dagger in my heart.

"Don't they argue in the car? Get antsy?" I asked, my eyes pleading for a lie to assuage my despair.

"No, not really. They enjoy looking at the scenery. They're pretty mellow."

The preceding anecdote should sufficiently explain why this woman is now a "former friend." Who could withstand this kind of peer pressure?

In our family, the concept of "togetherness" definitely has its limits. That's why we have labored to discover some particularly wily solutions to the dilemma of the family vacation. One clever trick we employed was to take separate vacations. No, my husband didn't go to Acapulco while I hit the slots in Vegas; we split up the kids. We arranged it so that our four children were never all in the same enclosed travel vehicle for more than a few nanoseconds at a time. This meant that we actually put our two oldest ones on an airplane when they were only seven and nine years old and flew them up to California's Bay Area to stay with friends, while we drove up Highway 5 with our youngest children. Since they were three and a five years old at the time, this car ride through California's agricultural belly offered plenty of excitement. We never knew when we'd see another convoy of trucks carrying enough tomatoes to drown the entire state of Nevada in marinara sauce. And, just when things threatened to get dull, we'd pass thousands of blasé cows standing or lying around, obviously counting out-of-state license plates.

My husband and I were happy campers. It didn't bother us in the least that we had to endure Raffi belting out seventeen rounds of "Baby Beluga" for six straight hours. We knew that for the relatively small price of two round-trip air tickets from L.A. to San Jose, we had cut the potential for motorized hostilities by more than half. We also figured we'd added a year or two to our life spans, due to our enhanced emotional stability.

This was a win-win situation, and I highly recommend it. Our little kids were happy, since they got to go to the bathroom in every junction from Bakersfield to Barstow and 132 other places in between. They were also rewarded for good behavior (defined as not asking "Are we there yet?" every forty-five seconds) with junk food from the mini-marts where we both emptied and filled our tanks. And our oldest boys felt quite grown up, flying the friendly skies, and getting to order any soda they wanted under the nonjudgmental eye of a kindly flight attendant. And, when we all eventually met up at our friends' home after an entire day's separation, we were moderately glad to see one another.

However, not all our out-of-town friends are so generous as to collect our children from the baggage claims of airports across the nation, so we often revert to Plan B: Stay home. Or at least don't go far. Living in Los Angeles, this is pretty easy. We can drive only an hour or two to the mountains or the desert, and feel like we've gone someplace new.

But when the kids are very young, planning a vacation entails knowing several critical things. First, does your vacation spot have a children's museum? Because God knows, no kids' vacation is complete without a chance to dress up in a fireman's (oops! I mean firefighter's) slick yellow pants, jacket, and oversized helmet. We proudly claim title to the nation's largest collection of miniature firefighter photo-ops snapped at every *farshtunkeneh* kids' museum from Pasadena to Paramus. Take my advice: Skip the one in Pasadena and go directly to Paramus. Theirs is much better. My idea of an ideal vacation spot is a place with a great big outlet mall. But nobody asked me.

Long ago and far away, when we had just one child whom we still carried in a baby backpack, we thought it safe to venture into a museum in San Diego containing not sand art but actual oil paintings by dead white European males. Unfortunately, the attendants were not thorough enough in their security procedures.

During our visit to this repository of priceless art, they asked us to turn in our camera, but they did not think to ask for our son's large plastic Cookie Monster toy. Nor did we think that Cookie Monster presented any clear and present danger to the museum collection. However, as we stood in front of a sixteenth-century landscape recently purchased from a Sotheby's auction, our son unexpectedly hurled Cookie Monster right at the painting. Okay, so the landscape wasn't the best in that room, but we chastised him nonetheless for his inexcusable breach of museum decorum. Of course, our hearts were pounding relentlessly—we could never have afforded to replace or even repair any damage our budding art critic might have done. Fortunately, the closest museum attendant at the scene of this crime had turned his back at a very opportune moment for us, and his ear piece had prevented him from hearing the "ping" of Cookie Monster hitting the landscape. The toy also bounced back to us so we didn't even have to reach under the rope to retrieve it. Anyway, I don't think anyone will notice that little nick by the river.

Now, when your entire family travels by plane, as we have done on a few occasions, make sure to allow plenty of time (I recommend three days) to get from home to the airport. Minor emergencies are sure to arise. Few things are more stressful than sitting in the perpetual traffic snarl choking the airport, watching the minutes to your flight departure tick inexorably away. Trust me on this one; I know.

The first time we traveled to the East Coast before Thanksgiving, the busiest travel time of the year, we did NOT leave enough time to get to the airport. The results were harrowing. My husband finally got us to the curb at the airport, whereupon I hurled each kid and his or her luggage out of the van, in a desperate "Hail Mary" play learned from the NFL. When we finally had all disembarked from the car, my husband snaked his way toward the end zone of the long-term parking lot and then ran like hell back to the terminal. Each child, even our 2-year-old, had to schlep her own carry-on, since there is no way to pack lightly when going from a warm to cold climate with young children. (Our baby's suitcase carried Essentials of Life: blankie, doll, penguin, mini M&Ms, and small travel set with fat crayons and cardboard canvases.) Lines to get through security were unbearably long, and I feared that we might miss our flight. I unsuccessfully tried to hide my panic, and once through the metal detector, I had to drag the littlest kids as fast as their short legs could carry them to gate 72G, which was at the far end of the terminal, naturally.

Since everyone else but us had boarded, only a few seats remained on the flight, and certainly there was no single aisle to accommodate a family of six.

"What do you mean, we can't sit together?" I said to the attendant. "What am I supposed to do, put my 2-year-old next to a stranger? Can't you see if anyone would volunteer to move so we can be with our children?"

But no, this was too much to expect. At least our 4-year-old became quite chummy with his seatmate.

"Where are you going?" my son asked his new acquaintance.

"New York," the man replied.

My son was astonished at this remarkable coincidence. "Me too! Did you bring your special pillow and blankie?"

"No, I'm afraid not," answered this indulgent soul, who entertained my son's prying questions from Los Angeles to Wichita, Kansas, at which point he pretended to be asleep. For the rest of the trip, though, my son worried about this man. He simply couldn't imagine anyone traveling without these precious items. To him, it was like being deprived of oxygen.

My daughter did not become chummy with the very unlucky woman in front of her. She was frustrated beyond anything she had endured in thirty-two months of life on this Earth by being strapped into her car seat on the plane, and took this frustration out by continually kicking the seat in front of her. I was mortified. It was one of those Parent Moments From Hell, when I realized that short of trying to score some thorazine from a doctor on board, there was little I could do. Sure, I held my daughter's legs down until she screamed (about 0.3 seconds) and offered a pathetic, insipidly apologetic look on my face every time the woman shot me a blistering look of hate. Fortunately, the flight was only five-and-a-half hours. It could have been worse; we could have been crossing the Atlantic.

My oldest boys nabbed two seats together where they played electronic poker and struck up conversations with other strangers about the prospects of the Lakers beating the Knicks.

My husband lucked out and scored a seat so far from any of his family that he could plausibly pretend he had never seen us before in his life. But every hour or so, I walked over to him, reintroducing myself and suggesting it was time for us to switch seats because it was his turn to grovel apologetically to the passenger our daughter was assaulting with her small feet.

Funny, I can't remember much about the actual trip once we landed. Something about the Empire State Building comes to mind, and I have a fuzzy recollection of some well-lighted Christmas decorations along Fifth Avenue, but I was too busy counting heads to see much at or above my eye level. We also went to someplace my daughter called the "Statute of Liberty," where she remarked in frustration that New York was no fun because there wasn't anyplace to jump around and really enjoy herself.

Come to think of it, if that's what would have made her happy, we should have just gone to that kids' museum in Pasadena.

Chapter 15

Working? Out of the Home???

I don't often feel like physically assaulting another member of my gender, but one time I had difficulty subduing what sociologists now call "rage."

At the time of this almost-crime, I had been a stay-at-home mother for nine years. My husband and I had decided when our first child was born that I would give up my job as a publications editor at a large health care company and freelance from home. I did this fairly regularly until one day I found myself with three little boys aged four and younger and I began to have trouble stringing together more than three coherent sentences at a time.

Once I recovered from this stage, I hungered for work again. So when a friend asked me to fill in as his publications editor while he looked for a new one, I jumped at the chance. After all, it had been years since I had a reason to put on lipstick and a nice dress every day, or hang around the big copy machine and wait for some fresh and tantalizing gossip to waft by the Mr. Coffee pot.

After I had figured out the logistics of childcare and car-pooling, I began my work as a "temp." The work was fun, mildly challenging, though not up to the level of responsibility I had enjoyed years before and relinquished in favor of full-time motherhood. A few weeks into the assignment, I walked into "my office" one morning to find a young woman planted there. I gathered that she meant to stay. She had decorated the place by fanning out a display of her favorite magazines, which had names like *Edgy*, on the credenza. I didn't recognize her, and discovered I felt alarmingly territorial.

I introduced myself, and politely asked her to state her business.

She then introduced herself as the new editor. No one had told me my days of looking out a big fifth-story glass window were about to screech to a halt.

"Oh, I see," I said as pleasantly as possible. Even though I didn't want this job permanently, I took an instant dislike to this interloper. She had an attitude, typical of the very young, not to mention black nail polish and lipstick in a creepy shade of brown. And if her display of *Edgy* magazine was any kind of statement, I suspected that her moral compass had swung wildly off course. The only thing the man on the magazine cover wore was a surly expression and hair sculpted into something that looked like dangerous implements. The article titles advertised on the cover contained many unrepeatable words.

"Well," Ms. Edgy said, "this job must really have been a feather in your cap."

In case you haven't guessed, this is the part where I really wanted to punch her lights out.

"Oh, is that so?" I said, getting in her face. "It just so

happens, you little info-babe wannabe, that I was charging executive lunches on my company American Express Gold Card when you were still dabbing Clearasil on your zits. And it just so happens that I did this job as a favor for a friend. I used to hire and fire entire editorial production staffs back when you were bumming cigarettes in your scummy high school bathroom hoping not to get suspended by the principal. Meanwhile, I've been doing really important work, specifically, raising children. And, as for your own taste in publications," (here I gestured dramatically toward her magazines), "that is NOT how one spells the word *fornicate*."

Ms. Edgy did not respond. This is because, in all honesty, I didn't say any of that. But I thought it, and only good breeding, instilled by my parents, prevented me from spewing forth my venomous feelings.

I can't remember exactly what I did say, but if this saucy scullion had the perceptive powers of a Q-Tip or higher, she would have absorbed the meaning of my withering glare. After staring her down for what I hoped was a sufficiently humbling period, I stalked out of the office and into the bathroom, where, to my horror, I discovered that the hem of my skirt had come undone. I had stormed away from this black leather, miniskirted malignancy dragging a trail of thread behind me.

I spent the next half-hour in the bathroom, taping my hem back in place with a roll of tape I had filched from a secretary's drawer. In the bathroom, I vowed never, ever to accept office work again without first double-checking every seam in my wardrobe.

Other than coming undone that day, both at the seams and at the nerve endings, I'd had fun at my temporary editing job. After all, I'd enjoyed a great view from the window. I also liked pawing through the generous assortment of teas and hot chocolates set out in the kitchen. Oh, yes, and the pay wasn't bad either.

Neither did I have the distractions and worries of working from home, such as having one of my progeny answer the phone and tell my client that I was "making" and couldn't talk right now. Since this child always hung up without asking the caller's name, I was never sure in front of whom to be embarrassed. This kind of thing is an occupational hazard for parents working from home. Once, for example, I answered the phone while holding a toddler in the other arm—a usual and customary practice. This, too, was a business call, and no sooner had my client and I exchanged pleasantries than my daughter unleashed a mammoth belch into the mouthpiece of the phone.

"That wasn't me!" I cried in alarm. "That was my baby. See, I'm holding her, and she just drank a lot."

"Oh, that's quite all right. I understand," my client said. Was that a wariness in his tone I detected? Or just my own hard-earned paranoia? Even though we kept working together, I always wondered if he had believed me, or if he thought I was an irredeemably vulgar lush with a penchant for spotting dangling participles.

Another time, a client came to the house in the early evening, when everybody was home. This young man had a slight build, extremely long hair and an earring. So of course two of my children circled him, posselike, and studied him. "Are you a boy or a girl?" one of them asked, as my husband ran forward to whisk them out of the room.

Needless to say, a business contact with whom you have played phone tag for two weeks will undoubtedly finally reach you at the worst possible time. When I had only one baby, I did regular freelance work that demanded many lengthy phone interviews with people in far-flung time zones. Sure enough, just as I was about to feed my hungry infant one evening, a man I had been trying to reach for days finally called me—from Indonesia.

"Certainly I can talk now!" I chirped, wondering how on Earth I could keep my baby quiet for a whole thirty minutes. I swept him up in my arms, plopped him down in the middle of my bed, looked at him sternly and whispered, "Don't move!"

My poor baby just stared at me, bewildered. "What happened to my meal?" his expression seemed to ask. Feeling guilty for shunting him aside, I conducted the world's fastest international phone interview while constantly looking over my shoulder at my baby to make sure he wasn't about to roll off the bed.

Ten years later, this same child suffered further neglect at my working-from-home hands. It was late in the evening, and I was interviewing a client. My son came over to me with a grapefruit, a plate and a knife and asked me to cut the fruit. I mouthed to him that I was busy and that he could cut it himself. So, while I continued to chat merrily with my client, my son went back to the kitchen. Soon I heard him yell something about blood. At first I didn't pay much attention, since experience had taught me that his definition of "bleeding" was about as accurate as Ralph Nader's claims that green leather upholstery in SUVs causes cancer. But darned if he didn't keep yelling, and I finally put my client on hold and went to the kitchen. I then realized that my son had cut his hand with the knife and *was* bleeding. Heavily. Guilt-wracked, I wrapped his hand in a towel, picked up the phone just long enough to shout, "My kid's bleeding. I'll call you later!" and then sped my son to the emergency room to get stitches. I tried not to think about the fact that by just stopping for a minute and cutting the fruit myself I could have prevented this injury.

I've always laughed at women's magazines that featured articles on how mothers can work effectively at home. You've seen them; they have these absurd photos of a mother sitting at her (neat) computer desk, her ear clamped to the phone, and her toddler sitting serenely on her lap as she works! They must use sophisticated digital processing to create this kind of shot, superimposing a photo of a happy and contented baby onto this woman's empty lap. Because let's face it, no baby who isn't sleeping or drugged will sit in front of a computer keyboard and not start jamming the keys with all her might.

Still, I know that no office environment is glitch-free, and I don't regret having plied my trade from home for these many years. Besides, I have moved up in the world, even in my home office. When I first became a mother and we lived in a tiny condo, I somehow squeezed a computer table into the corner of our Lilliputian bedroom and worked there, fending off agoraphobia at the same time. A few years later, I graduated to a larger corner of the living room, where I sat wedged between the wall and the sideboard. But the living room at least afforded a window view—of the toys and wagons in the backyard. Only recently have I joined the big leagues of working at home: I have my own office. Yes, I actually commute to work. Coffee cup in hand, I fight the morning traffic in the hallway, encountering occasional gridlock by the laundry room, and pass through the back door of the house. I go down the steps and take eleven strides to my office in our converted garage. Here I have an enormous desk—clearly a rebellion from my years of sitting at desks the size of a phone booth.

But here, at least, in the privacy of my own office, I have no fear of young, churlish editorial trespassers wearing black nail polish.

Chapter 16

Too Creative for My Own Good

I know a woman with seven children and an immaculate house. To my mind, these two facts should be mutually exclusive. But in her case, they are not. Running her house with military precision enables her to make a part-time career out of organizing the homes and offices of normal people. And why shouldn't she? After all, she doesn't have to devote twelve hours a week looking for mislaid bills and kids' homework assignments, so she's got time on her hands.

I viewed this woman with one part obsession, two parts suspicion. How did she do it? I pondered this one day as I emptied my entire pantry, hunting for a box of baking soda that somehow had ended up in the freezer instead. How could anybody with kids keep a household so precisely ordered? I began to suspect she had Germanic ancestors. On the other hand, I thought, how could anyone find fulfillment alphabetizing spices and ironing name labels on the inside of underwear? The fact that she still wore a size six after all those pregnancies didn't help either, let me tell you. Therefore, I think I can be forgiven for seeing little potential in any future relationship with her.

Until a certain Thursday, that is, when I realized that I had spent five of my six available work hours just searching for things. Not hard things, like the meaning of life, or the instructions for the VCR, but simple things, like the folder with all my notes for a current job project, postage stamps, a pen with ink, and a pair of matching socks.

That was a dark day in the annals of my work-at-home life. I couldn't erase the image of Darlene, snappily dressed by 7:00 a.m. (having no doubt laid her clothes out the night before), dropping her kids at school by 8:30, and at her first appointment by 9:00. Meanwhile, I had accomplished absolutely nothing by 3:00 p.m. except for having dangerously accelerated my blood pressure. I needed to leave soon to fetch my offspring, and I couldn't even find my car keys.

By this time, I was frazzled, frustrated, and frighteningly forlorn. I had to face facts: I needed help. By the time I reached for the phone to call her, my hands were shaking. I would have to swallow my pride along with the last of my M&Ms and call Darlene. Trying to look on the bright side, I thought it would help build my character.

I sloshed in my work boots through the avalanche of flotsam and jetsam (a.k.a. my "home office"), picked up the phone and punched in the number. A perky message greeted me.

"You have reached the neat and tidy office of Darlene's Home Systems Management. I am either on another line or picking up the clutter from someone else's workspace. Please leave a message and I'll buzz you back promptly!"

I gripped the phone, took a breath, and said, "Hello, um, um, I'm a little nervous about anyone seeing my house, but please call me back. If you don't, I'll probably never find your phone number again."

In a few minutes, Darlene called me back. When she heard my trembling voice, she modulated her tone to that of a suicide prevention counselor.

"Really, don't worry! Everybody has special talents," Darlene said. "Mine is organizing. What are yours?"

I explained to her that I was a writer, and that I could make a mean pasta primavera.

"Aha! I could have guessed. I make most of my money helping writers. You just seem to think differently from the rest of us. You're so creative."

I felt much better.

"But listen," I said, "this is a big job, a really big job. Can you promise confidentiality? I wouldn't want it to get around just how 'creative' I really am! Ha ha!"

"Everyone's nervous their first time," Darlene assured me. "Don't worry. You can write me an anonymous testimonial on plain paper—no letterhead."

"Deal."

"How's Thursday at 11:00?"

"A.M. or P.M.?" I asked.

"A.M."

"Fine," I said, scratching down the time on the underside of my M&M's packet. "See you then."

Thursday morning at 9:00 a.m., I began to panic. Although Darlene was coming to help organize me, I was too ashamed to have her see my home office au natural. I decided to clear off my desk. I quickly dispensed with the top five inches of material on it. This hodgepodge included: a wedding invitation from a couple who had recently divorced; cereal coupons that had expired in the previous presidential administration; a parental consent form for last month's field trip; a WANTED poster with my picture released by my local library announcing the revocation of my library privileges (the clincher was when I lost the volume "How to Organize Your Life in Six Easy Steps"); and a summons to post bail for failure to pay a parking ticket. How could I have paid it when I didn't know where it was?

And then I found the really important stuff: my frequent buyer card from Baskin-Robbins (only two shakes left till my freebie!); my rental coupon from Blockbuster Video; the appointment card for my next haircut, and two cubes missing from my Boggle set.

As I scurried around trying to tidy things up, I heard a knock at the door. Of course, it was the stroke of 11:00. People who are neat are also annoyingly prompt. My heart pounded with the humiliation that awaited me.

I looked with despair around my disheveled domicile. My floor was buried under a blizzard of bills, an avalanche of arcana. I should have applied to FEMA for disaster relief. Tripping over my son's skate, I went to answer the door.

Adding insult to injury, Darlene was immaculately dressed, coolly coiffed, clipboard in hand. She sailed into the house and took in the sight, catching her jaw as it began its freefall descent. It could have been the wreckage from the *Titanic*, if that great ship had served on Corelle. Seeing my home, Darlene's face conveyed the kind of pain that could only have been felt by the fiendishly methodical. I suspected this might be a clinical condition, and probably not even her fault.

"Well," Darlene smiled—a little stiffly—"we certainly have our work cut out for us. Where would you like to start?"

Sheepishly, I pointed to the confetti of chaos strewn over my floor. Darlene nodded solemnly. She examined my current "filing system," which until that moment had been a piling system, and began making a list of office supplies on her notepad.

Don't ask me what happened during the next two hours. I was nearly blinded by the speed with which this one-woman organizational SWAT team sorted out my sordid mess. Faster than you could stamp the words "final notice" on a phone bill, Darlene had transformed my desk: bank statements were clipped in chronological order, notes from a dozen different writing projects awaited my attention in color-coded files, the stapler had been refilled, pens stood at attention in a nifty round canister.

"Well," Darlene said with a touch of pride, "what do you think of this desk now?"

"It's great," I said. "Whose is it?"

It took a few days to absorb the shock of my new, orderly abode. Granted, the rest of the house still looked like Hurricane Georges, but one small island of calm had emerged. There was one problem, though. I wasn't sure I could write in such an uncluttered environment. I decided to give it a try. I made the happy discovery that my productivity went up when I spent less time excavating junk in a fruitless search for project notes that somehow ended up in the hamper (don't ask). Also, I received fewer abusive notices from bill collectors now that I could find my bills and pay them.

Still, old habits die hard. That's why I've got Darlene on retainer. Every few weeks or so, she comes over to help me clean up my act. And while she's straightening me out, I make her some pasta primavera for lunch.

Chapter 17

Stretch Marks: Every Mother's God-Given Right

E verything in a woman's life changes when she becomes pregnant. Her appetite rocks and reels. Some days, she is insatiable, possessed with demonic force by the notion that only a double pastrami burger with a side of nachos stands between her and insanity. Even the mentally deficient understand the foolhardiness of getting between an expectant woman and her food. Though few people know it, most of the female guests on the Jerry Springer show are pregnant women, kidnapped just as their forks were poised to attack a steaming bowl of fettuccini Alfredo. Millions of Americans with far too much time on their hands have seen the ugly results.

Other days, a pregnant woman can be minding her own business at work, when suddenly a co-worker in the next cubicle will make the mistake of thinking about a tuna melt for lunch. Meanwhile, the pregnant woman, exhausted and green around the gills, has spent the last twelve days doing nothing but sucking saltine crackers and sipping seltzer. She will instantly march over to that co-worker, sensing his offending thought, and demand, "Stop thinking about FISH, will you? You're making me sick! Do you want me to upchuck all over your third-quarter reports?" This is the co-worker's subtle hint that he had better think less threatening gastronomic thoughts.

During my pregnancies, I have also been gripped by incredible fickleness in the food department. During one pregnancy, I simply had to have barbecued chicken that came from a particular, inconveniently located restaurant. My husband offered to drive a dozen miles out of his way after work to bring it home for me. I couldn't wait to get it, couldn't think about anything other than eating that heavenly barbecued chicken. I paced the floor in anticipation of when my husband would arrive home with the goods, my hands shaking with ravenous desire.

When he finally came home, though, I didn't lunge for the insulated bag holding my bird. Instead, I lunged for the bathroom, because the smell of the dinner I had been crazed for all afternoon now made me so sick that I couldn't bear to be in the same apartment with it. I felt so guilty, having sent my husband on a fool's errand. I forced myself to sit down at the table, and even cut a tiny piece of the meat, but it was no use. I wanted to eat this about as much as I wanted to drink bilge water.

The appetite isn't the only thing that zigzags. A pregnant woman's energy level can also drop from sixty to six in a matter of seconds, and she will need some serious hibernation with her womb for days on end. But, perversely, just as she is largest, most ungainly, and seemingly least able to manage it, her energy surges. This well-known "nesting" instinct seizes her, and compels her to strip wallpaper, retile the bathroom, and carve radishes into the shape of tulips. I'm convinced that Martha Stewart would be an ordinary person today if not for the fact that her nesting instinct went into overdrive more than twenty years ago and never deactivated. But not everyone can build an empire by rhapsodizing over cheesecloth and instructing people on how to stencil their own living rooms.

Though pregnancy is temporary, normal mothers will live with reminders of their expectant state for the rest of their days. I say "normal mothers" because I can't bear the thought of other women who somehow weaseled their way out of some of the more depressing after-facts of pregnancy.

One of the most dismal days in my life was the day I went to the hospital to visit my friend Peggy, who, just hours before, had delivered a strapping ten-pound baby. When I entered the room, Peggy was holding her newborn son and crying with joy. Within seconds, I too had dissolved in tears. Not because the baby was so cute or because the sight was deeply affecting, but because I saw that Peggy's abdomen was completely flat. Frankly, I don't recall much about the baby at all. Peggy didn't even have the common courtesy of appearing to have overindulged a little at an all-you-can-eat Sunday brunch.

What gives? I thought. Certainly not her taut, rippled abs. This may explain why the only case of postpartum depression after that birth was *mine*.

In retrospect, I've tried to turn this cruel inequity into an enriching, character-building experience. When I think of friends like Peggy, I tell myself, "It's not her fault that she didn't show until a few days before she packed her bag to go to the hospital. It's also not her fault that despite being Italian, she was built with stealth Scandinavian genes, while I was assembled with eighteenth-century Polish DNA that is ever alert for the next famine. And I'm sure she won't take that ad agency up on its offer to pose for Calvin Klein jeans so soon after giving birth."

I often have reminded myself that true beauty is within, that our souls must be beautiful. Unfortunately, I generally succumb to less generous thoughts. When I see fair-skinned, blond string beans with their young, I am cheered to think that unless they are using sunblock with an SP count of about 120, their porcelain flesh will wrinkle much more dramatically, and much earlier, than my olive complexion. Sometimes, I am disturbingly buoyed by the thought that as the more slender women age, their physical deterioration will come as a greater shock. After all, I will have had decades longer to brace myself.

Believe me, I don't like being shallow. But sometimes it's a survival strategy. And it comes in especially handy when my kids see me sitting on the couch, poke a finger into my navel, like I'm the Pillsbury doughboy, and ask, "Is there another baby in there?"

Now, as a general rule I don't pick arguments with the Almighty. But seeing as He is the one responsible for the research and development of this whole Reproduction Division in Humanity, Incorporated, I don't think it would have been too much to ask for a little Divinely-inspired instant liposuction during the delivery.

It's not as if we are likely to forget that we have children unless we still carry around a little spare tire all the time. Are we supposed to look down at our elastic-waist jeans and say, "By golly, I did have a baby eight years ago! And here's the proof!"

And would it be too much to ask the nurses in the ob-gyn's office to refrain from clucking their disapproval after they order you onto the scale? Can't they muster a liitle more sympathy? If I were the doctor, I would train my nursing staff to say, very apologetically, "I am grievously sorry to ask you this indelicate question, but would you mind getting on the scale? I promise to instantly forget the number."

Because no pregnant woman likes getting on a scale. Now, even if the nurses had asked me like that, and even offered to then fall on their syringes, my answer would probably still have been the same: "Scales are for fish."

I've tried to look on the bright side of all this. Once, on a visit to the zoo with my kids, I realized that a nine-month pregnancy wasn't that bad, considering what some of our friends in the animal kingdom endure. Most mammals, like chimps, deer and other primates, wait it out for about seven to nine months, just like women. But lots of animals spend more than a full year in a delicate condition. And elephants? Fuggetaboudit! An expectant elephant spends nearly two years in the family way and delivers, on average, a 225-pound baby. But even elephants get a break: I have it on good authority those pregnant elephants "hide their weight very well." Furthermore, postpartum animals slip effortlessly right back into their pre-parturient wardrobes. Luckily for them, they don't need to start measuring or weighing their daily allotment of grass or hay to shed those unwanted pounds.

Although I try to be charitable, as my zoological research must prove, I still don't understand—nor appreciate—how some women can spend nine months eating enchiladas and drinking strawberry milkshakes, gain fifty or sixty pounds, and then POOF! They dispose of the evidence as fast as a drug pusher flushes thousands of dollars of cocaine down the toilet when the cops drop by. Meanwhile, those of us who gained twenty or thirty pounds less are still lying about our weight on our drivers' licenses, twenty-three years after we have given birth. I still have nightmares about those magazine covers with Demi Moore and Cindy Crawford, both naked and great with child. Yeah, those were really helpful. And you wonder why women can be so catty.

These moms have all the excuses. My friend Zena looked the same at six weeks postpartum as she did six weeks preconception. "Oh well," she offered by way of apology, "you know, the baby is nursing all the time, which really takes the weight off!" People like Zena cannot understand what the rest of us know: that the sleaziest four words in the English language are "one size fits all."

Others claim that because their babies never sleep for more than thirty-eight minutes at a stretch, they are up burning calories round the clock.

I don't buy it. I've nursed my kids for a combined total of nearly five years and the only thing I lost was some more distance between sea level and my breasts. I've also done several tours of round-the-clock duty with newborns, but my thyroid gland saw no reason to get excited. I believe that my thyroid is actually a member of the little known but powerful AA-SBG, or Amalgamated Association of Sluggish Bodily Glands, a subdivision of the AFL-CIO. Their motto is: "We don't work overtime."

So I'm still trying to make peace with my maternal figure. I remind myself that mothers have made important strides in nearly all professional fields. We have fought for and won the right to elbow our way into previously male-dominated territory. Now it's time to add another to our roster of entitlements: stretch marks—every mother's God-given right.

Chapter 18

Pyramid Schemes

During my quest to make peace with my body, I have fought quite a few skirmishes. Once, for example, I arrived back at my car after shopping at a Toys 'R' Us only to find a flyer on my windshield that read, "Lose Weight Now! Ask Me How!" It reminded me of that old TV commercial where a poor unsuspecting guy with bad breath gets a note from "The Green Phantom," warning him that only a particular mouthwash can save him from permanent social exile to Twin Forks, Idaho. I tore the flyer from my windshield and whipped my head around, looking for the perpetrator. Was this message spammed all over the parking lot, or had I been carefully selected after some thorough market research? Of course, I would never know, but the fact that you are paranoid doesn't mean they aren't out to get you.

This stealth advertisement held no appeal for me. It was just another come-on, like those advertisements for bad diet products with names like "Fats-Off!" and the diuretic, "Leak to Sleek." I began to wonder: Where were all the responsible medical researchers? Why weren't they helping us? The answer was clear: They were out there doing the 100,000th study on the long-term effects of smoking (clinical result: "DUH!").

We women continually serve our country by relinquishing our bodies for a full nine months at a crack to bring forth the next generation. Is it too much to ask that our country throw a billion here or there to find a way to do what "Thin-Thin" did, only without the heart valve problems? Why is there no Division of Cellulite Studies at the National Institutes of Health? Is this not sex discrimination of the highest order?

Nutrition researchers have a lot to answer for. After all, they can't make up their minds about what we should eat, when to eat it, and how much. I grew up in a house with a shelf groaning under the weight of dozens of diet books, all of them fraudulent, and with wacky names to boot. Even as a kid, I tried dozens of these schemes, including the 747 Pilot Diet; the Water Cooler and Frito Fat-Off; the Tijuana Taco Trimmer; the Chili Burger and Celery Slimmer; and the Guava Pit and Guacamole Gut Gouger. In this last one, the key to permanent and successful weight loss was to eat only the guava pits, supposedly a hotbed of nutrients with calorie-ripping properties. You saved the guacamole for a subsequent facial mask.

After chubby adolescence, I finally pared myself down without the benefit of any diet book. After absolutely no scientific research, I devised my own regimen, which I called the "Pizza and Frozen Yogurt Diet." I thought this was a logical name since these were the two basic food groups comprising the program. I maintained this arduous eating plan rigorously throughout four years of college and a year of graduate school.

Sure, it was tough, but I was on a mission. Still, years later, pregnancy packed the weight back on.

When my first child was born, carbohydrates were all the rage. I went to the gym to work out, and studied the posters along the walls, all showing King Carbohydrate at the broad base of that inviolable food pyramid. The svelte and obscenely fit exercise instructors swore by this philosophy: Carbs were GOOD! Protein was BAD!

So I began making a lot of spaghetti dinners. And I all but banished protein from our plates, because the Food Pyramid had commanded me that Carbs were GOOD! Protein was BAD! So I carbo-loaded, and pound-loaded at the same time. I couldn't help wondering what was wrong with me, why my body wasn't cooperating with a plan endorsed by the nation's top minds in nutrition.

Then, I'm driving along one day, listening to the radio, when I hear a doctor talk about his new book "The No-Zone," which proclaimed a new weight loss truth across the land. And what was this truth? That carbohydrates were BAD! Protein was GOOD! I had been DUPED!

I gripped the steering wheel tightly to avoid hitting oncoming traffic. You cannot imagine my despair upon hearing this news. After years of making the pasta du jour because the "experts" told me, I had learned at a busy intersection (already infamous for its high rate of accidents) that carbohydrates were evil incarnate, the nutritional equivalent of Agent Orange! And protein, which I had shunned like so much radioactive waste, was really my dietary savior. I didn't know which was worse, the scientists' galling certainty that this time they had gotten it right, or my own gullibility.

But one thing was certain: No one was giving the straight skinny on becoming a lean, mean, mommy machine. Ever since my first son was conceived and hijacked my figure (and I do blame him—he's an easy target, and he never makes his bed) I've been trying to get it back. Subsequent pregnancies only delayed this mission, and I place the blame for this squarely on these subsequent children's heads.

Of my numerous efforts to release my thin physique from captivity in a chubby body, perhaps none was more foolhardy than the time I visited a psychologist who had reputedly developed a super program for weight loss. You see, this psychologist, Dr. Anne O. Rechsic, was so thin that her dress size barely qualified as a prime number. And you know, thin people have this really annoying way of making thinness seem so natural. Dr. Rechsic's plan was called "Eat Me, I'm Yours!" In her office, she explained how it worked:

"Judy, it's simple. Just listen to your appetite. Think of what you really want to eat, and then go eat it! Don't eat when you're not hungry, and don't eat any foods that aren't pleasing."

"You mean, I shouldn't finish my kids' cold chicken nuggets so they don't go to waste?"

"Well, where would you rather see them?" she asked, tearing off a piece of smelly green sea kelp from a plate on her desk. She daintily bit into it, creating a low-cal crunching sound. "In the garbage disposal or on your hips?"

Dr. Rechsic had a point.

"So," I continued, wanting to get really clear on this concept, "if I don't eat their leftovers, and only eat what I really want to eat, when I want it, does that mean I can eat sweets?"

"Yes! If you really want them!" she enthused. "I have at least three cartons of Haagan-Daz in my freezer all the time!" she said. As she spoke I noticed that her belt was buckled on the tightest hole. "I eat it whenever I want to!"

Hmm, I thought. I, too, had several cartons of Haagan-Daz at home. Only mine were in the garbage, because they were empty.

I left Dr. Rechsic's office, swelled with the kind of fulsome inspiration that is ultimately very short-lived. I wanted to follow her instructions on the "Eat Me, I'm Yours!" plan, but one of the conditions of this program was to use my imagination and think of foods that would not just suppress my appetite, but provide me with an incredible culinary delight. That way, she said, I would feel far more satisfied with less. If I wanted beef Bourguignon, I must make it! If I decided I must have chicken Kiev, or cherries jubilee, I must make it! I should not settle for that tuna casserole with rigor mortis in the back of the fridge simply for economy's sake, because that would not be ultimately satisfying.

The only kicker here was: What mother of young children had time to make cherries jubilee or chicken Kiev? Still, I made a valiant effort. That afternoon, I devoted a half-hour to deep contemplation about what I felt I "must have" for dinner that night. When I discovered it, I put my kids in the car and went to the market to gather the ingredients. I came home with my elbow-shaped pasta and fresh cheddar cheese, and began making real macaroni and cheese—from scratch.

But as I gently stirred the cheese sauce while listening to the evening news, a reporter announced a new study linking excess dairy consumption with breast cancer in women. Now this was a horse of a different color. Weren't they also drumming into us women that we require busloads of calcium to save our bones from osteoporosis? And last time I checked, weren't dairy products one of the best sources of calcium? What were we supposed to do, chew on antacid tablets all day long? Suck on oyster shells?

I had trouble enjoying my macaroni and cheese that night. Not because the crust wasn't perfectly browned and the macaroni itself bubbled to perfection, but because as I ate, I heard the nagging voices of "experts" giving completely contradictory advice:

Eat whatever you want!

Don't you dare eat whatever you want, unless what you want is a three-ounce portion of grilled skinless, boneless chicken breast!

Eat dairy products!

Don't eat dairy products!

Take multivitamins!

Don't take multivitamins unless you're sure the formulation is pure!

Take an iron supplement!

Be careful what kind of iron supplement you take, or you'll get constipated!

Eat lots of carbohydrates!

No, don't! Eat lots of protein!

Carbs!

Protein!

Carbs!

Protein!

And on and on. Needless to say, I quickly dropped out of the "Eat Me, I'm Yours!" plan and went searching for a more realistic scheme. I next turned to my friend Gina, who suggested I see her food counselor. The counselor made Gina write down everything she ate, when she ate it, and how much she enjoyed it on a scale from A to Z, with A being abominable and Z being, I guess, zippity-doo-dah, zippity-ay. This sounded okay until we got to the catch: I would also have to give up a single food that was my downfall.

"Give it up? As in forever?" I gulped.

"Well, maybe not forever," Gina said. "Some people are able to begin eating their 'downfall' foods again after two or three years."

I nearly fainted from joy. I told her I'd give it some thought, and snuck off to ponder this over a dish of leftover macaroni and cheese.

I even got as far as writing down what I ate, and when, and how much, and my score. But when I needed a calculator to tally the day's calorie count, and found that it exceeded the day's Dow Jones Industrial Average, I began to feel feverish, and I had to lie down.

So, as I watched Gina peel off pounds, I tried my next gambit: drinking water. Supposedly, drinking at least eight glasses of water a day would help you lose weight, detoxify, clear your acne, raise your IQ and lower your tax bracket. Maybe this was the ticket. It certainly sounded like the least painful way to get my figure back. So first thing in the morning, I drank as much water as I safely could before the forty-five minute round-trip drive to and from the kids' school.

I drank more when I came home, and continued to drink through the morning. I quickly realized that drinking eight glasses of water a day is a full-time job. It's not the actual drinking that takes so much time—it's the ensuing "detoxification" that follows that drowns your day. Every time I tried to do a simple task, such as make a bed or call Information, I had to stop in the middle to go to the bathroom so I could lose another three or four ounces of excess water.

Men usually don't have this problem before age sixty. And women who haven't given birth may never have this problem. This brings us to one of the many abounding paradoxes of motherhood: A woman is somehow built to carry around a growing baby in her womb for nine months, but after she delivers she can no longer carry a morning cup of coffee in her bladder for more than fifteen minutes.

I've concluded by now that every diet plan is really a racket. And, once you've read through all the sizzling promises that consume the first 200 pages of any diet book, you arrive at the inexorable clincher: Losing weight means one thing and one thing only—three ounces of skinless, boneless chicken or turkey breast and a side of "veggies." You can't even afford to eat the rest of the letters of the word "vegetable." You're on a diet, so you can only afford to eat "veggies." I really hate that word. It's like saying "undies" instead of underwear, or "oopsies" instead of "lawsuit." This is all well and good if you are addressing a kid, but when a book or magazine article writer is speaking to me as an adult, I would appreciate hearing the whole entire word.

Anyway, do you know how little three ounces of skinless, boneless chicken is? Do you know how little three ounces of anything is? You can figure it out easily by using another diet come-on: serving yourself meals on small plates to "trick yourself" (as if you are that stupid) that you are really eating more!

So when my daughter invited me to a tea party with Physicist Barbie and her sidekick, Beaker-Washer Ken, I tested this idea. We took our best Fisher-Price tea party china, and sure enough, my allotment of chicken filled the whole plate! Cutting the meat with toy cutlery also took a half-hour, by which time I was too tired to eat. As for my "veggies," I loaded them in the matching teacup and was overjoyed to see them fill it to the brim. Indeed, my cup ranneth over.

I could go on, but I have another chapter to write. Let's suffice it to say that I have drawn my own food pyramid, and

I'm pretty certain it works. The tip of the pyramid is guava pits. Slightly below that is the section for skinless, boneless anything. The mid-section of the pyramid is reserved for fruits, vegetables, and whole grains.

The foundation of them all, supporting that entire pyramid, is composed of pizza and frozen yogurt.

Chapter 19

Carpool Tunnel Syndrome

M*y Ford is their Shepherd; they shall not walk.
They maketh the seats recline back at green
  lights;
They lead one another in carpool contention,
They disrupteth my soul;
They guide me to their friends' homes for
  their play dates;
Yea, though I drive through the battle of traffic
  congestion,
I will fear no evil,
For school is nearby.
The playground and classrooms, they comfort me.
They straggle out from the car dragging backpacks;
I can now go get coffee; my latte runneth over.
Surely safe driving discounts shall follow me
  all the days of my life,
And I shall drive around town in my Ford, forever.*

I was sitting in the dental chair, a fat wad of purple modeling clay stuffed in the southeast corner of my mouth. I tried not to think of why I might have deserved this fate, lying semiprone in a sad excuse for a lounge chair, feeling haplessly undignified in my little blue bib. I glanced at my watch, and realized impatiently that *Gone with the Wind* wasn't nearly as long as this visit to the Drill-'N-Bill Dental Center. By this point, my gums weren't the only things that were irritated.

I moved the little table chock full of dental instrumentation out of my way and swung myself out of the chair. I pried the modeling clay out of my mouth, signaled to my dentist, who was working in the next cubicle, flashing a laser over someone's uppers. I said, "Ah leafing."

Enunciation is much easier after the novocaine wears off.

"What are you doing?" he said in alarm. "I told you the impression needs five to eight minutes to set fully. You don't want us to have to do it a fourth time, do you?"

"Yuh fy minuth ith over. Ah leafing. Ah haf cahpooh."

"What?"

"CAHPOOH! Kidth! Thkool!" I said, and, needing to display a sense of self-empowerment that belied my Daffy Duck speech, I ripped the blue bib off my neck.

"Oh, you have CARPOOL! Why didn't you say so earlier?" The dentist became instantly sympathetic. "We'll work with this impression, then. I'm sure your crown will be fine. Run along now. Shirley!" he called to the office manager, "Mrs. Gruen has CARPOOL! Don't bother her about the bill today. Just send it to her in the mail."

Not all dentists are this understanding, mind you. Especially since the Drill-'N-Bill Dental Center posts a sign in the waiting room that states clearly, "Payment is extracted when services are rendered." But as this true-life example shows, carpool can take over a mother's life as nothing other than pregnancy can.

One might not think that the job of ferrying children to and from school, sports and music practices, and other appointments would loom so large in the motherhood scheme. But trust me, once kids are on the school and after-school activity circuit, a mom's life becomes a seven-day-a-week game of beat-the-clock. Every activity, meeting, lunch date, medical appointment and chore suddenly revolve around drop-off and pick-up times. Many schools and day care centers also begin charging by the minute if you are late. Some of these after-school workers, I think, were parking enforcement officers in a previous life. They just can't wait to write you up when your meter runs out.

Outside of those nasty behind-the-scenes machinations at presidential conventions, nothing is as political, as rife with drama, as carpool. Friendships are forged and others broken irrevocably over a missed 3:00 p.m. pick-up. Divorces are rarely as messy as the dissolution of a long-standing carpool arrangement.

"Did I tell you what happened with Jan?" a friend asked me one day over a supermarket scrip purchase.

"No, what?"

"We're no longer speaking. She forgot to bring Ashleigh Caitlin home two weeks in a row on the Tuesday pick-up, and since I was at work Ashleigh Caitlin missed her ballet lesson and now she isn't eligible to perform in the recital."

"Oh no!" I gasped. "I had heard about Jan. I was warned not to carpool with her for just that reason. Monica told me that her son Leonardo also missed his semifinal basketball game when Jan spaced out of a 4:00 p.m. Thursday pick-up, and they're not speaking, either."

"Well, Jan made up some excuse, of course, but we both know the truth. She just didn't make it a *priority*."

I learned the hard way that mothers are loathe to throw a well-oiled carpool into disarray by introducing any new complicating factor. One summer, I switched my kids to a new school. It was ludicrously late to even attempt to find a carpool partner, but the thought of that several-mile trip each morning and afternoon without relief was enough to make me think the unthinkable: home schooling.

Once the kids were enrolled, though, my first imperative, even before checking out the uniform and book requirements, was to commandeer a copy of the parent roster and ingratiate myself into a carpool.

In my first dozen or so calls, I was treated with kindness and pity. "Oh dear, sorry, we made our arrangements last spring. But good luck to you. God knows you'll need it."

"You need a carpool now?" another asked, trying to hide her disbelief. Her tone reminded me of the old saying stating that a lack of planning on your part did not constitute an emergency on my part. If I am not mistaken, I may have also heard a hint of "Nyah nyah nyah nyah nyah, nyah!"

On my third call, I began to edge closer to a solution. The woman explained: "Well, I have an arrangement, but we may be able to squeeze you in. It depends on whether Lisa can change her daughter's after-school speech therapy to Saturdays, in which case I'll have room to take her son to his karate lesson on Wednesdays, but I really won't know that until Cheryl gets permission from her boss to arrive at 9:00 instead of 8:30 each morning. So basically I'll have to get back to you."

While trying to keep everyone's contingency plans

straight, I tried to squelch my fear that I'd be out of the loop completely. If I couldn't snag a partner, every morning and every afternoon, in sickness and in health, till graduation do us part, I would end up the sole cabbie, snack dispenser, argument arbitrator, and the only one to repeatedly insist that all limbs and phlegm must remain inside the car at all times.

I continued calling other mothers, my fate hanging in the balance. Meanwhile, I decided to get assertive. As a former P.O.C. (Prisoner of Car) and veteran of two years without a carpool, I dared not consider my precarious emotional status if I didn't get one now. I might even suffer a bout of post-transit stress disorder. So I decided to write a personal ad. My clock was ticking, and I was getting more desperate by the day.

My first ad read as follows:

Handsome 2-year-old minivan ISO same or SUV. Must enjoy leisurely drives in rush-hour traffic with numerous children and backpacks. Clean oil filters, excellent air pressure. Fit 3,000#. High tolerance for Teletubbie theme music and the Disney radio station. Drivers with full tanks only, please.

Sure, everyone worries about the unmarried singles these days. Newspapers and magazines feature pages of small-print ads trying to lure the DPM with the SOH and a passion for dolphins to his true love, who had better be slim, fit, tanned and ready for some power yoga if she had any chance for a LTR. But what about us drive-time singles? We may appear to be merely oversized vehicles plastered with boastful bumper stickers ("My child was Chalkboard Monitor of the Month"), but we're crying out for companionship, too.

No one, but no one, should underestimate the importance of carpool, or the emotional toll it takes on drivers. One morning last spring before school ended, I met my friend Diane for coffee after morning drop off. I got there first, and was savoring my Brazilian Vanilla-Cinnamon Decaf Sumatra when she arrived. I took one look at her and knew exactly what she'd gone through. Her expression could only be described as "terrorized."

"What happened?" I asked Diane.

"How do you do it each day?" she asked. "It's so exhausting!"

"You mean carpooling?"

"Yes! My God, just getting them into the car takes a half-hour! Who gets to sit in the co-pilot's seat, who can't sit in the back because that seat belt 'hurts,' whose arm isn't allowed to touch whose armrest. Then, once mine are all in I have to pick up the kids down the block. They take forever to get themselves in, and step on everyone else's backpacks, which sets my kids to complaining again. This morning one of them also regaled us all with how many kids threw up in class yesterday, how far everyone's vomit projected...thank God I hadn't eaten yet. I swear, I've only been up for an hour and a half and I need to take a nap already."

"I know what you mean," I commiserated. "Today my daughter cried all the way to school because she said her hair was too 'fat.' Two of the boys argued over whether the Mets have a chance in the World Series, and the youngest just kept kicking her brother's chair because he had taken the last juice box."

"What did you do?" Diane asked.

"I pulled over twice. The first time I made one kid get out and walk two blocks before letting him back in the car. The second time I pulled over so that I could take a walk down the block to clear my head. I was a wreck. It takes me at least half an hour to decompress after the morning drive. That's why I'm determined to get a carpool for next year. It's taking years off my life."

"Only seven hours till we have to go back," Diane said, trying to sound cheerful.

I realized it was no coincidence that Prozac gained its enormous popularity at the same time more moms entered the workforce, thus necessitating more hard-to-find carpool arrangements. Carpoolers-without-partners must be the least-recognized minority group in our nation today, second only to left-handed vegan Gulf War vets. Researchers are only now beginning to realize that the medical condition mitakenly identified as "carpal tunnel syndrome" is really "carpool tunnel syndrome." The primary symptom is an inability to ever see your way clear to an appointment at 8:00 in the morning or 4:00 in the afternoon for the rest of your life. Night sweats, migraines and nausea are not uncommon.

When my first ad failed as bait, I pulled out all the stops for my second ad. After all, desperate times called for desperate measures:

Rugged, shapely hunk of tanned steel ISO up to four additional short passengers for committed LTR through urban streets. Gorgeous chassis. DMV-tested safe. A.M. or P.M.— your choice. Unlimited snacks provided to all passengers. Can withstand whining up to sixty decibels. Will pay mileage and scrip requirements. Give us a test drive!

A bit overblown? Perhaps. But no more so than the thousands of bankrupt, boorish, follically challenged men and women out there who claim to be "sophisticated," "good looking," "witty" and "financially secure," while searching for love at a few bucks per line. Anyway, I was willing to do more than my fair share for this relationship.

Believe it or not, I had to turn down the two people who answered my second ad. One had been postmarked near the prison in Lompoc and the second demanded an exorbitant finder's fee for an introduction to someone known only as "Smokey."

Just when I was about to indulge my despair in a pint of Ben & Jerry's Chubby Hubby ice cream, the phone rang.

"Hello? My name's Shauna? I'm the one who laughed when you called me a few weeks ago about carpool? I told you I was all set? Well, um, I just got a call and I lost my afternoon carpool? Are you still available?"

Well now, the shoe was on the other accelerator, wasn't it? Once a pariah, I was now in demand. However, I wasn't sure whether I had confidence in a carpool partner who wasn't sure if her name was Shauna or not. And she *had* laughed when I called—very poor form. Still, I couldn't really afford to play hard to get in mid-August. We made a date to compare our kids' school, tai kwon do, creative drawing, therapy and tennis lesson schedules to see if we were compatible.

And I'm happy to report that two other mothers also ended up calling, in breathless urgency, when their carpool partners ditched them at the last moment. Finally, I was in the driver's seat, so to speak.

By the time school started, I had learned that it's always darkest before the driveway, and I was able to tell my doctor that I wouldn't need that Prozac refill after all.

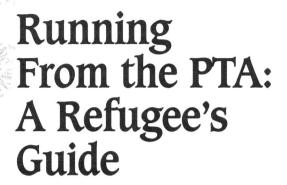

Chapter 20

Running From the PTA: A Refugee's Guide

One of the many benefits of answering machines and voice mail is that you can bypass a lot of calls that you otherwise would have regretted taking. Who knows how many new fire insurance policies I would own if I hadn't stopped picking up the phone during dinnertime?

But sometimes, in a moment of folly, I inexplicably sweep that phone off its base and innocently say, "Hello?" instantly opening myself up to requests like this one:

"Hi Mrs. Gruen! This is Phyllis from the school PTA calling, and I'd like to remind you that you signed up last September to be a room mother for your first-grader's class. Do you remember this, Mrs. Gruen?"

They were slick, these PTA moms.

"Uh, yes, of course I remember, Phyllis," I say, wondering which of my weekdays would suddenly vanish.

"Wonderful! Well now, with Thanksgiving coming up, we

were hoping that you could come help your son's class make a pot of Pilgrim Soup this Wednesday at 1:00 p.m. Can I count on you?"

And so that is how on Wednesday afternoon I became the sous chef of the first-grade class. And, because the teacher only had a small, child-sized plastic knife and paper plate to offer me, that is why by 2:30, my fingers were aching from the effort of cutting, peeling, and chopping raw vegetables as hard as Plymouth Rock. However, the children, who were making heroic efforts to cut the vegetables with the same limited culinary instruments, had a marvelous time, particularly when small bits of potato went flying off the table, bonking a classmate on the head.

Anyone who has ever tried to peel, cut and slice raw vegetables with only a plastic knife and a paper plate knows why the food processor was invented. As soon as the vegetables were cut, the harried teacher dumped them into her pressure cooker so that the kids could enjoy their soup before the bell rang at the end of the day.

"Here Mrs. Gruen, have some!" the teacher offered graciously after the cauldron had bubbled for some time.

"No, sorry, I'm parsnip-intolerant," I apologized. While the teacher's back had been turned, I had witnessed one roguish child pick up several stepped-on vegetables from the floor, and fling them into the soup. "I've got to run along now! It's been fun!"

Of course, after all was said and done, and my fingers stopped aching, I was glad to have helped out my son's class. Kids get so excited when their moms or dads come to school for reasons other than to retrieve them from detention.

But I didn't feel quite so noble the next time I was reminded of my PTA commitment.

"Hello Mrs. Gruen! This is Phyllis from the PTA calling again! I just want to thank you, SO MUCH, for helping out with the Pilgrim Soup project. Now as you know from the school newsletter, it's almost time for our annual chocolate sale, and I was wondering if you would sell some World's Finest Chocolates on the yard after school next week. Any day is fine."

"Well now, that depends," I said.

"On what?"

"Would you like to have any chocolates left to sell by the end of the day?"

"Well, no, if you're that wonderful a salesperson, we'd be thrilled to have you sell out the stock! My gosh, if you can do that, I can probably get you named as Chocolate Chairperson for next year!"

"No, no no!" I cried. "You misunderstand me. You see, chocolate and me, well, we have kind of a dysfunctional-enabling kind of relationship. I'm afraid it might be too tempting for me to sit there surrounded by all those fine chocolate bars and not, well, eat some."

The silence on the other end was just long enough for me to understand that my standing in this woman's eyes had plummeted to several leagues under the sea.

"Mrs. Gruen, I cannot believe that any mother could even fathom eating the proceeds that our school so desperately needs to revamp the science library!"

"I suppose we really don't know each other very well, then," I said. "Of course, I'd pay for anything I ate, but I hate to put myself on the front lines of temptation."

Another pause.

"I see." Here Phyllis emitted the kind of sigh that suggested she had had to shoulder just a tad too many of the world's problems that day. Given her cavalier attitude toward my chocolate "problem," I guessed that she was probably the type whose idea of a calming respite after a grueling day was to steep some herbal tea and recklessly splurge on half a tea biscuit. "Well, then, I'll just sign you up for the spring magazine drive instead, okay?"

"No, wait!" I shouted, but it was too late. Phyllis had hung up on me and my chocoholism. It wasn't really her fault. She was just trying to do her job. I realized that these PTA moms, toiling away as volunteers for the good of the school, were among the last unsung heroines in our society. But that didn't mean I was prepared to sing in the chorus.

I thought about calling her back and succumbing to the siren song of the chocolate drive, but I felt that I would no longer be trusted to sit alone at that table. Someone would undoubtedly get tapped to monitor me, perhaps even train a video camera on me, and frequently "drop by" for surreptitious inventory counts of those World's Finest Chocolate bars and a peek in the till. I had my pride, after all.

As much as I feared an afternoon staring down all those chocolate bars (which would undoubtedly include the dark chocolate, bittersweet chocolate, chocolate with almonds, and my favorite, the milk chocolate with the crispy centers), I really did not want to get corralled into the magazine drive. Or the book sale the month after that. Or the mother-daughter breakfast after that. Or the recycling drive after that.

It was endless, this PTA business. I respected the mothers who worked so tirelessly for the cause of the school, but really, wasn't there an easier way to raise a few thousand bucks over the course of the year? How many chocolate bars would we really have to sell before we could even dust off the science lab, let alone revamp it?

I would rather dust it myself than go around to the neighbors, asking, "Sure you can't use a subscription to *Cat Fancy*? You do have a cat, don't you?" Or have to run after the mail carrier waving the magazine subscription form in my hand, begging, "*Philatelic Monthly*! Only $12.90 for sixteen exciting issues!"

Of course, the children are supposed to do the selling, but we moms know better. We end up doing the selling because our kid is so excited by the prospect of winning the prize—you know, that cheap disposable camera that she'll get for selling sixty-four magazine subscriptions in forty-eight hours. So we moms are the ones who shamelessly hit up our parents, our second cousins who we haven't seen in thirty-two years, and even the checker at the grocery store. With a pathetic and obsequious smile on our faces, we go begging. "*National Geographic*? No, already have it? *Brides*? Oh, right, you're a 'groom'. Okay, how about *Bag Boy Bazaar*? Oh, am I holding up the line here? Sorry, I'll just be running along now."

It made me sound manic, and just as aggressive as Phyllis and all those other PTA ladies who call, knowing that when they do, I somehow won't let voice mail pick up. If I did, they'd only call back. These women never take "no" for an answer.

Anyway, I think I've learned my lesson now. When the kids get home from school and it gets close to dinnertime, I give the phone to one kid and say, "Hide it. Don't let me know where it is. I don't want to know who's calling."

And when magazine drive season rolls around, I just go out and buy my kids the darned disposable camera myself. I figure it's a whole lot cheaper than ruining my reputation in the neighborhood.

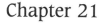

Chapter 21

The Great Escape

I remember a great scene near the end of the movie *Terms of Endearment*. In the movie, Jack Nicholson (a retired astronaut) was forever trying to get away from Shirley Maclaine, who had this habit of always nabbing him when he was trying to go someplace, such as back to NASA for one more joyride. In this scene, Jack is at the airport, luggage in hand, when Shirley reappears, perhaps just returning from a past life, and collars him in a new moment of distress. In his inimitable style, Jack mutters, "Just seconds from a clean getaway."

That's how moms feel all the time. We're forever trying to get out of the house—it doesn't matter where—and our kids are like Shirley Maclaine, materializing out of nowhere, clinging barnacle-like to our legs, telling us how much they need us. Situations like this fall somewhere between a Kodak moment and a Prozac moment.

So I was pretty excited to receive an invitation to a

women's overnight retreat. According to the brochure, this retreat was geared for women who needed "fun and spiritual enrichment." I had never done anything like this before. After eleven solid years of motherhood, I leaped at the chance.

But, like Jack Nicholson in the movie (I do believe the similarities stop here), I was just seconds from a clean getaway when my daughter started trailing me like a Secret Service agent assigned to the presidential detail. I was throwing the few things I needed into an overnight bag, but everywhere I tried to step, she was there.

"Why are you going, Mommy? Can I visit you? When will you be home? Can I use your nail polish? Why are you getting dressed so fancy?"

"She'll be back tomorrow. SHEESH!" said my oldest son, who had apparently joined the detail. "By the way, Mom, can you leave early to come watch my basketball game?"

"Step aside, kids," I said. "Time's a-wasting. It may be another eleven years before I get to do this again. Outta my way!" The whole retreat was less than twenty-four hours; I had to make every minute count. As I opened the door to leave, my husband asked me when I'd be back. I was intentionally vague.

"Gee, I'm not sure. Sometime tomorrow night," I said, closing the door behind me. I had heard from women who had attended the year before that although the event ended in the afternoon, a number of women gallivanted about town for the next several hours. They took in a museum, luxuriated in a restaurant where they enjoyed a dinner they hadn't cooked or served themselves, or simply hid in their cars around the corner from their houses, afraid to reenter.

In my haste to sidestep my children, to whom love and devotion meant blocking my every move toward the door, I forgot my carefully packed toiletry case at home, and had to call the hotel bell captain at midnight for a toothbrush. It was a small price to pay for eighteen hours of R&R.

When I checked in at the hotel, the retreat organizers handed me the schedule of events. I thought to myself, who needs this? I had an electronic card key to get into a room where no one would bang on the bathroom door a nanosecond after I went in there and demand, "What are you doing in there, Mommy?" I had a separate key for the refrigerator mini-bar. I had brought a good novel, and the hotel offered forty-seven movie channels. As far as I was concerned, I had already gotten my money's worth.

Almost all the attendees were mothers—who else felt such a compulsion to run away from home for a night? After our dinner on an outside patio, we had a good old-fashioned sing-a-long and discovered that we still remembered the words to "If I Had a Hammer," "One Tin Soldier," and "Puff the Magic Dragon." If only we had been wearing our tie-dyed T-shirts and our teenagers' bellbottoms, we would have experienced total déjà vu.

During the chorus of "You've Got a Friend," one of the organizers set up an ice cream sundae buffet, proving to me that these people were really professionals. "Winter, spring, summer or fa-aall," I sang, squeezing chocolate syrup over my low-fat ice cream, "all you've got to do is CAA-AALL," reaching for some whipped cream, "and I'll BE THERE, YEAH, YEAH, YEAH…." This was my kind of party.

The next morning, we were scheduled for some serious interpersonal enrichment. So after breakfast, we gathered in a conference room where Dr. Karma, a psychotherapist, invited us to get comfortable in our chairs or on the floor. Her mission: to help us experience a new kind of openness, an enhanced spiritual connection, and bring our center points to a new level of clarity. At Dr. Karma's request, we closed our eyes and listened to soft New Age-y background music as she led us on our spiritual journey:

"Let your mind wander, and feel the problems of everyday life float up and away. . . ," Dr. Karma murmured in a gentle tone I imagined was usually reserved for speaking to the dangerously psychotic. "Take yourselves on a journey to the most beautiful place you've ever been. Imagine yourself in this place of unparalleled grandeur and serenity. It could be a forest, a mountaintop, a beach. Try to center your spiritual self there. Release your mind and soul to the possibilities..."

I cheated, opening my eyes and noticing that most of the women had already zoned out in Xanadu. I wondered if I could sneak out and hit the gift shop without being noticed. But then I saw Dr. Karma looking my way, so I quickly shut my eyes, like a kid pretending to be asleep when her parents peek into the room.

When the exercise was over, Dr. Karma asked us to share with the group the places we'd gone. A woman across the room raised her hand immediately. She seemed upset. "I feel awful!" she said. "You see, I first chose the south of France, where we went on our honeymoon. But then I thought of the Japanese tea garden in Golden Gate Park, and then the conflicts began: France or San Francisco? San Francisco or France? I couldn't make up my mind. So I didn't get centered, since I was constantly struggling to find my place. I'm sorry," she apologized, with an expression that suggested she had failed some sort of critical exam.

Dr. Karma oozed sympathy. "None of us are used to the luxury of being alone with our own thoughts. It takes practice and commitment. Here, take my business card," she said to the woman. "We can set up a schedule so I can help center you on a regular basis."

Then another woman raised her hand. "Did anyone besides me choose a place that included her children?" The rest of the women burst into laughter immediately, and their laughter gathered force like a hurricane off the East Coast, becoming uncontrollable. It took Dr. Karma quite some time to settle the women down.

Then I did something dangerous. I yawned and stretched, which Dr. Karma mistook for my volunteering to share with the group. She called on me to tell everyone which beautiful place I had selected for my spiritual awakening.

"I, too, had a conflict," I said honestly. "First I was in the shoe department of Nordstrom during the semiannual sale, but it wasn't serene, since there was a lot of pushing and shoving to get to the Enzo Anglioni display, so then I took myself to Bloomingdale's. But Nordstrom kept calling to me, and then Bloomies. I just couldn't decide: Nordstrom or Bloomies? Bloomies, or Nordstrom? So I also failed at finding nirvana, since I was paralyzed by the burden of overchoice." I tried to look contrite as I said this.

Dr. Karma shot me a steely stare. "I'm sorry if your center point is a hub of mindless materialism," she said, pointedly not offering me her business card. "Perhaps it might help you if you read my new book, *Recriminations From Women Who Shop Too Much.*" She then turned to the next woman, which was fine with me, because I sure as heck didn't appreciate her glib put-down of that cherished American institution, the high-end department store. Besides, I didn't think I could take much more spiritual enrichment in a single morning.

I had lived in California too long to expect that this program would improve, so I picked my mindless materialistic self up and took a walk until the next item of interest: lunch.

Despite my run-in with Dr. Karma, I enjoyed being away from home. And I was completely engrossed by the post-lunch activity, a presentation by a holistic physician on herbal remedies for PMS and menopause. I mean, how often do women have a chance to gather for a powwow about their options for cramp relief? The air conditioner seemed to fail us that afternoon, so I wasn't sure whether my hot flashes were "sympathy pains" for the older women among us, who were speaking out about rather sensitive female topics, or just annoyance that I had missed the waiter whizzing by our table with a second pot of coffee.

To keep our interest during the presentation, one of the retreat organizers, Sherry, promised to raffle off two huge gift baskets later that afternoon. Sherry's exuberant tone implied that the lucky winners would cart off a prize equal to the Hope Diamond. I looked over and saw the enormous baskets, light glinting off their colorful cellophane wrapping. My heart quickened as I wondered what could be inside: a cornucopia of exotic cosmetics samples? Dazzling new lipsticks, perhaps, and a splash of heady cologne? Dare I imagine a tasteful piece of jewelry?

See, every time I have a chance to buy a raffle ticket, I buy. I never win. Intuition told me that this day would be different. I was feeling lucky.

It was hard to get the women out of that room, though, engrossed as we all were in debating the merits of evening primrose oil versus blue cohosh as a remedy for bloating. I, however, knew I had heard enough when the doctor, a woman who made my daughter's Physicist Barbie look fat, insisted that indulging cravings for chocolate during "that time of the month" was a terrible error that would only aggravate our other symptoms.

Frankly, she had already lost all credibility with me by admitting that she didn't even like chocolate in the first place. How could she possibly understand the gravitational force field that pulls women to chocolate, stronger even than the force pulling men toward television during the Super Bowl? I pulled my retreat schedule out from my bag to see what was next, while focusing my spiritual center point on winning one of those baskets.

Our next activity was a jazzercise class, and boy, was I ready. That is, until I saw the instructor. She was all sinew and gristle, and as she spoke, moving her arms and legs so as to burn as many calories as possible per second, I could see her muscles tone themselves. Her thighs had more definition than Merriam-Webster's dictionary (unabridged). She then introduced herself.

"Hi! I'm Bobbie, I'm forty-eight, I've got three grown children and two grandchildren, and I only started working out ten years ago. I used to weigh 192 pounds and my idea of exercise was doing menu lifting repetitions at restaurants."

I stared in wonder at this paragon of physical perfection as Bobbie continued.

"Now I'm a triathlete and on the side I run a highly successful dotcom company. Sorry I'm a little late, but I just came from teaching my morning spinning and aerobox classes. I want you all to know that exercise can change your life!"

Was it my imagination, or was Bobbie looking at me as she made this claim?

"Now, is EVERYBODY READY?" Bobbie started bouncing and strutting as she pressed the tape player, which immediately blared out Bruce Springsteen's "Born to Run."

As I jumped, leaped and otherwise pranced about, utterly failing to keep up with Bobbie's graceful movements, I marveled at the conference organizers' uncanny ability to pack the program with instructors who so effectively made me aware of my own inferior spiritual awareness, lack of holistic understanding and limited physical stamina. I began to think that I should have followed my first impulse and ditched the entire thing. If I really had wanted rejuvenation, I should have stayed holed up in my room, flipping cable channels and ordering room service.

Still, if Bobbie could go from bakery hound to bicep babe and look like that at her age, perhaps I should reconsider. During our third set of squats, Bobbie let it be known that she was available for hire as a personal trainer, so after class, drenched in enough sweat to top off the Dead Sea, I took her card.

I had no desire to attend the last scheduled event of the retreat, a community quilting project. Heck, I even take clothes that need buttons replaced to the tailors; I didn't think I'd stand a chance with high-concept arts and crafts. But I was in a pickle: They were going to call the winning raffle tickets for the baskets, so, reluctantly, I went.

Now, even as a kid, I had felt an aversion to crafts activities. Perhaps it's because I never graduated past the stage of being mesmerized by the sight of my fingerprint pattern lifted from a thin layer of glue. Perhaps it's because even my paint-by-numbers pattern of a little girl holding a puppy turned out like a Picasso, with the girl's eye landing on the dog's tail and the colors bizarrely off course. To call me "artistically challenged" was a compliment. I wish it had occurred to me to apply for a grant from the National Endowment for the Arts.

With less than an hour to go till my Great Escape ended, I joined the great spiritually centered sisterhood for the community quilt project. I stood in line behind an eager bevy of women who carefully studied and then chose from a vast array of fabric paints, strips of lace, sequins, buttons and fabrics laid out on the table. As usual, I sought the easy way out, finally settling on a swatch of fabric that I could just cut out and iron on to my patch of the quilt.

As I walked back to a table to construct my great work of art, I couldn't help but notice that the other women had unleashed a wellspring of creativity. These women were painting, sewing, and gluing their hearts out. They took buttons of varying shapes and colors and transformed them into peacocks, vineyards and mother-and-child motifs. I looked askance at my poor little swatch of fabric, glued slightly askew on my square of the quilt. I imagined the response of people who would look at it one day as it hung in the local community center:

"Gee, look, Marge, isn't this beautiful?"

"Oh yes, and isn't it nice that they included some work by the mentally challenged!"

"Where?"

"See? That patch there. That one couldn't have been done by anyone of normal intelligence."

No, I couldn't have that on my conscience. So I decided to get fancy by adding a lace border to my fabric. I watched others ironing on their appliques, using the special iron-on paper to get the job done. They made it look so easy, I thought even I could do it.

I studied their methodology, wanting to get it right, while I waited for my turn at the ironing board. It felt strange to actually hold the iron, an instrument with which I was not on the most intimate of terms. Just then Sherry announced that the big moment of the raffle drawing had arrived. She closed her eyes, dug her hand into a small drum, and pulled out the first ticket. She called the winning number, and a woman ran up to receive her prize, still holding a tube of fabric paint.

"Congratulations!" Sherry beamed. "You are the winner of this beautiful basket filled with herbal remedies for PMS symptoms!"

The winner, inexplicably crestfallen, politely thanked Sherry and returned to her table with enough herbs to open her own pharmacy.

"Humph!" I thought. "Good thing I never win anything at these raffles!" and concentrated on ironing my lace border. But when no one claimed the next winning number, I put my iron down and checked my ticket. Sure enough, I had won. I walked over to claim my basket of PMS remedies, but I was in for a surprise.

"Congratulations to you too!" Sherry said. "You have just won this beautiful basket full of menopause relief symptoms!"

Needless to say, I got completely choked up.

For a crazy moment, I wondered about the expiration date of the remedies, but it didn't really matter. I was feeling older by the minute. If I saw any more impossibly youthful, thin, and Olympian instructors during this retreat of "fun and spiritual enrichment," I would break out in menopause by the time I got home.

I set my basket down on the table and tried to complete my lace border for this interminable project. I expected to see the lace border firmly adhered to the fabric, where I had ironed it, but it wasn't there.

Only when I turned the iron over did I realize that I had heat sealed my lace, now shriveled to a fraction of its former self, to the face of the iron.

I dumped my quilt square into the garbage, took a fresh

one, and sat down at the table. I finally had an idea to contribute to the community quilt. On my new square I wrote in fabric paint, "I finally got away from home to a 'fun' women's retreat and all I got was hormone replacement therapy."

Chapter 22

In Loco Parentis, Try Rattling Your Light Saber

Remember when we thought there were four seasons, called spring, summer, winter and fall? Or, for those in the Midwest, two seasons: winter and road construction? That was long ago and far away.

Kids make you realize that the four seasons are really ear infection, soccer, science project, and camp. Sometimes the seasons can overlap, and when they do, you may not be sure if you should be wearing a sweater or cleats. Some seasons are insidiously long. If you are not careful, soccer season will slip right into basketball season, which then becomes freehand drawing season, and before you turn around it's soccer season again and you realize you have been parked at the same spot in the local recreation center for a solid year.

It's a toss-up which season is the toughest. Many a mom begins cursing Albert Einstein during science season, when we are expected to hunt for obscure materials to enable our kids to create a model of a gangrenous foot. We head over to Spores 'R Us and find green mossy material that the young scientist can slap onto the mold she has cast of Mom's foot. We stay up late, helping to type out tomorrow's report—the one that Clementine has known about for four weeks but "just remembered" that day.

Still, the toughest season for my money is summer, that overly romanticized netherland that arcs between school and summer camp. Parenting magazines really beat us up when it comes to summer, blaring know-it-all article titles at us to help us cope:

123 Crafts You Don't Want to Make with Your Kids This Summer!

The 30 All-Time Best Kids' Museums That You'll Never Visit This Vacation!

459 Boredom-Busters for Kids on Ritalin!

12 Kid-Friendly Cupcakes You Can Make with Wheat Germ!

Listen, I've given it the old college try. I dug out old T-shirts for a tie-dye project, but the kids decided to body paint instead. This wouldn't have been so bad, but the body they insisted on painting was mine. In today's twisted art world, I could have been hijacked as an exhibit, but the museum housing me would surely have been boycotted by conservative political groups.

I packed picnic lunches to take to new and beautiful parks that I discovered through extensive research, but the kids ate them in the car and claimed starvation before we arrived.

I dragged them to museums only to hear them complain that museums are useless because "you're just looking at stuff."

My default position in any pinch like this is a trip for ice cream.

This always gets everyone excited, as the kids know I'm a sucker for that old butterfat-sugar combo. And, more often than I should admit, I let them play computer.

Once, on the first day of school vacation, I discovered an eerie silence in the house. I seized the opportunity and called my friend Marilyn to see how she was coping so far. When she answered the phone, I heard crashes, shrieks and general mayhem in the background.

"Hello," she said in that barely even tone that mothers resort to when their children are home during the holidays.

"I guess I don't need to ask how you are," I said, feeling her pain.

"It's only been four hours," she said. "What am I going to do for the next eight weeks?" I heard something shatter in Marilyn's house, and it wasn't her nerves, either.

"Have you tried Ritalin?" I suggested.

"I already asked my doctor. He said the kids don't need it."

"I didn't mean for them."

"Hmmm. That's a thought. At this point, I should qualify for a prescription of some kind," Marilyn said. "I'll call the doctor back. Say, why's it so quiet on your end?"

"They're on the computer, playing 'Space Aliens Meet the Mafia.' They've been there since last Wednesday," I said.

"Do you have any plans for tomorrow?" Marilyn asked.

"Other than holding onto my tenuous grasp on sanity, not much," I answered. "I had plans for us to go to the Natural History Museum and the Imax today, but the kids spent an hour arguing over who had been the first to declare that a gross idea. After they got tired of that, they went skating for about two-and-a-half minutes and then came home to fight over the remaining orange juice. I was still trying to haul them into the car when my middle child tried to actualize his dream of being an only child. That's when I gave up and turned them over to the computer. Do you think an 8-year-old can get carpal tunnel syndrome?"

"I don't know," Marilyn sighed. Just then, a blood-curdling scream ripped through the phone lines. "Gottago!" she shouted and hung up.

Next I called my friend Audrey, who had earned my undying admiration years earlier. In the face of unspeakable whining from one of her children, Audrey had had the presence of mind to say to the child calmly, "Thank you for giving me the opportunity to practice being patient." Audrey read all the latest parenting books and often foisted her fresh ideas about being a better parent on unsuspecting friends like me.

Her youngest child answered the phone. "Whoozis?" she greeted in a squeaky voice.

"Hello, is your mother home?" I asked.

"MOMMY!" the child screamed into the mouthpiece of the phone, busting my ear drum. I switched the phone to my remaining working ear.

In a few moments, the kid came back and said, "She put herself in time-out in the bathroom. She won't come out."

I guess even Audrey had her limits. "I see," I said, worried. "I'll call back later. Thank you."

Unfortunately, I was unable to make any more phone calls, since at that moment my daughter had the temerity to actually breathe near her brother's face—a clear violation of his airspace and perhaps even of the NATO rules of engagement. In response, he caused Equestrian Barbie to take a hard fall, transforming her into Paraplegic Barbie. We then held an impromptu meeting to clarify our family rules for such activities as breathing, looking, smirking, making faces, pouncing, smacking, and, the most egregious offense according to my children, *copying*. We also discussed the proportional responses for each offense. I began to long for the snaking carpool line.

That night I did something really masochistic. I went online to check out airfares and to read the names of cities I might not ever visit in my life. I imagined what it would be like to dash off to New York, meander slowly through the Metropolitan Museum of Art and dine overlooking the Hudson River. I pictured Chicago's lakeshore, and imagined blowing smoke in a honky-tonk jazz dive. It didn't matter that I didn't smoke—the image of me, AWOL from the job of Mother, held romantic appeal. But my brain had been crisp fried to a crackly crunch that day, so even Fargo, North Dakota seemed exotic.

Camp was still two interminably long weeks away. I looked for more realistic succor in my parenting books. I picked up the perennial best-seller, *Siblings Without Stitches*, and reread it. I didn't understand why this was categorized as "Parenting." Clearly this was a humor book. (Make sure to see other titles in the same humor series, including *Warfare Without Weapons* and *Dieting Without Depression*.) These parenting methods always worked swell on paper. But when I tried some of those empathetic, reflective methods to let my children feel understood, they looked at me as if I were wearing a lampshade on my head and speaking in tongues.

Still, I was eager the next morning to make the day happy, or, at least, to prevent my children from accumulating any more disfiguring scars. I suggested we make Popsicle stick napkin holders that we could paint and decorate with glitter. Amazingly, the kids agreed, and all sat down at the kitchen table. But then we discovered that our glue had dried out, and the kids had no interest in going to the store to buy more.

They suddenly decided we must all see a movie, but argued over what to see: *Tarzan* or *Star Wars*.

Since I was the one with the car keys and wallet, I chose *Star Wars*, wishing as I did that I had my own high-tech light saber to restore order in my small empire. In an hour, we were at the theater. And for the next 142 minutes, there were no complaints (not counting whose turn it was to hold the popcorn and why people had to keep stepping over them to get to the bathroom). For a little over two hours, the only explosions were in a far-off galaxy. Peace prevailed with all my children around—this had to be science fiction.

Chapter 23

Be It Ever
So Humble. . .

When my husband and I married, we bought a tiny condominium. The condo's best feature was its Swiss chalet sloped beam ceiling. Painting it and the rest of the place all white convinced visitors that we had somehow sneakily added several hundred square feet to the place, but it was an illusion.

It was no illusion when, two children later, the condo had gone from cozy to claustrophobic. Our toddler son was on a search-and-destroy mission. We had to install a $300 security door—not to keep burglars out, but to keep him IN and to protect him from catapulting over our second-story landing. Meanwhile, our newborn son meant to test the patience and auditory responses of the entire zip code with his shrieks. Every day I waited for people from Child Protective Services to rap on my door and demand to know what in the world I was doing to induce such horrific screams from my baby. Then I'd have the chance to tell them the truth: I had gone to the bath-room.

When we moved to a rented 1,100-square-foot house nearby, we felt like we had landed in Trump Towers. "Look!" I said excitedly to my hubby. "I've been walking for fifteen consecutive seconds and I'm still inside!"

But when our lease was up, we bought an even larger home down the block. At the time, I couldn't imagine needing anything bigger: three-and-a-den, family room, nice kitchen. I unpacked to stay. Funny thing is, eight years and two more kids later, that same "open floor plan" that I had loved so much at first began to grate. It didn't matter where you were in the house; you heard every flush of the toilet, every blow of the nose. And, when we pulled up all the carpet to relieve my husband's allergies, you could have heard a bomb drop. And that's how it sounded each time a kid ran down a hall, dumped a backpack on the floor, or used the living room wall as a handball court.

You guessed it. I was ready to move "up" again, or at least to soundproof the house. Frankly, moving up sounded better.

"You realize how much money we've already put into this place?" the man I married responded to my idea. "We've repiped, rewired, painted, wallpapered, landscaped. We're staying."

"But we can hear everybody's bodily functions. We can never take a nap on Saturday afternoon," I said. "Don't you want to live in a place that's larger, and quieter?"

"You mean more expensive?" This seemed to settle the discussion from HIS point of view.

But not mine.

Maybe it was when I started shouting "What did you

say? I can't hear you with these ear plugs in!" Maybe it was when our dinner guests asked to use the bathroom—in the neighbor's house. Maybe it was the tape recording of the washing machine on the spin cycle and the sounds of sibling rivalry I planted in my husband's closet and played when he went to sleep. But whatever it was, his resistance fell. There are times when the ends must justify the means.

At the same time, real estate prices in Southern California were shooting up faster than a Silicon Valley splitting stock. I needed to work fast.

When we put our own house up for sale, buyers were so eager that they started storming the citadel two hours before the first open house was to begin. I was still balancing boxes of junk and picking up stray Monopoly pieces from the floor, trying to figure out where to hide everything when looky-loos barged in and began inspecting my linen closet. And, despite my having discovered a handful of Apple Jacks on the floor afterward, we sold our house during that first broker's caravan. Perhaps the cereal added to that homey feel.

We had to check our delirium when we began looking for a new house in our neighborhood of choice, where prices had galloped into the stratosphere. An Olympian on steroids would have had trouble catching up.

When I called a respected real estate agent who knew the ins and outs of my target neighborhood, she immediately chauffeured me around in her impeccably waxed BMW. I left my domestic Mom-mobile at the curb.

"So, how much have prices gone up since I last looked?" I asked my agent, still innocent.

"About a hundred grand," she said.

I swallowed hard, realizing that she did not mean rupees, shekels or lira. We were now talking about a kind of currency

I only felt comfortable spending when it had been printed by Milton Bradley.

"But I'm sure your home has gone up too," she said, feeling my pain through realtor osmosis.

"It has," I said, "but my home isn't exactly 'Beverly Hills-adjacent.' It's barely 'Marina del Rey-adjacent.' I just want to have a little more space, a little more privacy. Is that so much to ask for?"

Apparently, yes. Any house that we could afford had a catch, in the form of Real Estate Code, which I quickly mastered. For example, "cozy" meant that in a space contest between a telephone booth and a bedroom, the telephone booth would win. "Potential" was an ethereal concept, one that only someone with a hallucinogenic imagination might appreciate. And then of course there was every homebuyer's favorite: the homes needing "TLC" (Totally Laughable Condition). All of these potentially cozy homes cost much more than the home we just sold.

Under these circumstances, I might have been more forgiving after what happened when I allowed my husband to go look at a house with our realtor without me. He was so excited by what he saw, and especially its price, that he placed a full price offer on the spot.

Without my having seen it.

Now, if husbands really have a death wish, I can think of other ways to indulge it, such as hang gliding, a trek to Mount Fuji, or becoming a soldier of fortune. There, at least, they have a chance of emerging alive. But to buy a house without a wife's approval is perhaps the most reckless temptation of fate that I have ever heard of.

When he called and told me the happy news that we had just bought a new house, I was of course intrigued to learn a thing or two about it. I asked him about the location, which he said was "prime." I asked him about the kitchen. He said it had one, he thought, but he really didn't take much notice. I asked him about the yard. He said it had not only one level, but two. I asked him how many bedrooms it had. Three, if he was not mistaken.

Of course, when I saw the house, I realized my husband had been right on all counts. The house was in a "prime" location, along one of the city's busiest streets. You could walk to the market, the video store, and restaurants, and even better, you could throw out your alarm clock because the early morning commuters would start whizzing by your bedroom at the crack of dawn. It had a kitchen, and if you sucked in your breath, two people could turn around in it at the same time. The yard did indeed have two levels: the practical and the theoretical. See, the yard was a small patch of grass with a wide strip of concrete above it, the kind that kids like to balance on when they are walking down the street. This, apparently, was the "upper level" of the yard. And yes, there were three bedrooms, one of which could fit a small child and a hamster.

This was a watershed day in our marriage. We had an accepted offer on a house I hated. I sat down on the theoretical level of our new yard and cried. This was even more depressing than the day I saw that *Monica's Story* had hit the best-seller list.

"It was such a great price," defended my significant other, to whom I was lawfully wed. He didn't bother hiding his irritation at my ingratitude.

"It was such a great marriage," I said, watering the lawn with my tears.

After many obsequious apologies from our broker to theirs, and even an offer of hari-kari on all our parts, we weaseled out of the deal.

Thus snatched from the jaws of divorce court, I recovered my composure and redoubled my efforts to find us a new home. Something that was bigger than "cozy," easy on the "potential."

"I won't go down in size," I told our agent the next day. "My boys are growing fast. They need more room to wrestle and throw furniture at each other."

"Room to throw furniture will cost about fifty grand more."

"And what about kitchen cabinets? None of these kitchens have decent cabinets."

"You never mentioned cabinets," my agent said, checking the sheen on her nails. "Look," she said, "you want a bigger house, with cabinets, you're going to have to pay for it. Now are you ready to deal or not? I can't afford another debacle with you people." My agent was a busy person.

Seemingly, finding a home in this neighborhood was like ordering at a chichi French restaurant. Everything was à la carte: Closets. Yards. Cabinet space. I was hungry, but could afford only an appetizer.

"Not yet," I told her. "I've got to go home, drown my sorrows in a Godiva chocolate, which will soon be beyond my budget, and talk to my husband. I'll get back to you." My agent dropped me off in front of my domestic Mom-mobile and zoomed off to write an offer on behalf of A Serious Buyer.

At home, we sat down for a talk. Having been through several dozen homes already, I had seen enough brown drapes and orange carpet to last a lifetime. I dared not look at remodeled homes, the ones with Italian-tiled foyers. Though we wanted a home that was fully actualized, we could only afford "potential." We realized we had two options:

A. Buy a home that we liked in our target neighborhood despite the cost. It must be a home we really loved, because we would never be able to afford to go anywhere else ever again, perhaps for the rest of our lives. I would try to look beyond the fact that I would need to furnish it with couches dropped on the shoulder of the freeway.

B. Purchase the entire city of Cleveland.

Since neither option held great appeal, we struggled for creativity. We wracked our brains trying to remember any well-heeled elderly relatives on either side of the family who might need a "Just thinking of you" card. We started categorizing my husband's boyhood stamp collection, looking for an aged specimen that would make philatelic history and make our mortgage payments a heckuva lot easier. We looked for other hidden assets, such as a bank account in the Cayman Islands that somehow we had overlooked.

"Well?" My agent asked the next day over the phone. "Ready to write an offer yet? Properties are going fast."

"Not yet," I said, while concocting a recipe that involved day-old bread, rice and beans. Well, at least no more long lines at the butcher. "Give me another day. I think we might go for the house with the new tile in the kitchen and no yard."

"I thought you wanted a yard," my agent said.

"Look, I'm a realist," I answered. "We'll have a 'virtual yard' peeking next door. They have beautiful landscaping. By the way, would you buy a book titled *Living on Legumes*? I'm thinking of writing one."

"Dunno. What are they, some kind of tax-free mutual fund?"

"Never mind. Look, try to find me a house that fell out of escrow, the sellers have moved and are desperate to sell. Kitchen cabinets would be a plus. Can you do that?" I asked.

"Look, I'm a real estate agent, not a magician. But wait. I'm on the computer, and a new fixer just came up in your price range. You'll have to act fast. It's got a small yard, so it will probably go into multiple offers."

A few weeks later, we were delighted to find the perfect house: bigger than our old one. On a fairly quiet street. Okay, so with a fire station only two blocks away, we're among the first to learn of any new conflagrations in the neighborhood. No more open floor plan, so the house was more private and quiet—a condition that unnerved my daughter and made her insist that she could not sleep for lack of noise.

The house even maintained its "move-in condition" status for six full hours after we arrived. After that, it needed a paint job and some refinishing on the wood floors. But it was home. Our search had ended.

Our new house, despite its greater size, did have one thing in common with our old house: We could STILL hear everyone's bodily functions, except for discreet digestion. That's because after we moved in, we discovered that the place was equipped with the loudest plumbing fixtures in the history of porcelain.

However, the boys did have much more room to engage in mayhem and mischief, and isn't that why we coughed up the big bucks in the first place?

Chapter 24

"It's Like, You Know, Whatever"

My kids were having a discussion the other day. Well, "discussion" might be putting too fine a point on it, since it sounded like this:

"You know, it's like, that thing, you know, whatever!"

"What thing?"

"Duh!"

"C'mon, let's go, like, skating!"

"Whatever!"

Now, this is not a verbatim transcript, like the kind you can order from television news programs. Conversations in our home are never this congenial and rarely this articulate. Besides, no one in our family has ever experienced the unique sensation of finishing a sentence. How could they, when so many others are standing by, ready, willing and intent on completing it for them?

It's true. Communicating with kids is never easy, no matter how young or old they are. For example, when kids are still babies and learning to talk, they might insistently point to something and say "Thaaa!" You, the parent, are feverish with delight that your baby is such a genius, already saying "Thaaa!" when your friends' babies are still only saying "Pphluy!" Yet there is a problem, namely, you don't know what "Thaaa!" is. So you spend the next five hours, maybe the entire week, grabbing at objects all over the house, dangling them in front of baby's face, like Exhibit A in a courtroom drama, and naming them.

"Shoe? Is this what you want? Shoe? No? Okay, how about this? Is it this banana you want? No? Okay, how about your rattle? No? Not the rattle? Okay, how about this antique Ming vase? Is this what you want? No?"

While you, the parent, are working up a sweat, tearing around the house in search of that elusive object, namely, "Thaaa!" your baby is becoming increasingly frustrated, undoubtedly thinking to herself, "What is WRONG with these people? Don't they know that I want that pair of pruning shears over there on the coffee table? How did I get stuck with such nitwits for parents?"

As the years go by, communication gets even stickier. As soon as kids are old enough to state what they want, such as a $200 giant panda in the window of a toy store, or permission to dye their hair blue, they are still not old enough to understand why their parents are less than keen to help them fulfill these desires. This introduces conversations like this one:

"Why can't I go swimming now at Max's?"

"Because it's January and thirty-two degrees, that's why."

"SO????" the child responds, disdainfully rolling his eyes

at his parents' apparent cruelty and illogic.

"You could catch cold and get sick, that's why. It's not swimming weather."

"Nothing's gonna happen! I won't get sick!"

"Right. Nothing will happen. Because you're not going."

"That's so dumb!"

Or this one:

"Why can't I borrow the car tonight?"

"Because the last time you borrowed it you drove it till you ran out of gas, then had it towed to the nearest gas station, where you called me at midnight so that I could have the pleasure of driving over to pay for the towing as well as the gas. Does this register a blip on your radar screen?"

To which your child will reply:

"That's TOTALLY unfair!"

Kids just register information differently than adults. I think they must have some kind of "exaggerator" embedded in their brains. This exaggerator makes it impossible for the kids to relay certain messages without dramatic embellishments. So for example, if you ask your child, "Dear, would you please tell your sister and brothers to come to the dinner table now?" you can fully expect that your invitation will be transformed into an ugly threat, such as: "Mom says that if you don't come to the dinner table—RIGHT NOW—you're grounded for six months and won't be able to get your driver's license till you're twenty-one!"

It's no wonder that we moms must take our kids' statements with large hunks of salt. Because kids use the exaggerator in their reports to us, we mothers must counter by using our own special MotherFilter listening devices when hearing them out. Every mother has a MotherFilter listening device.

This is part of our psychological makeup, and is activated when our first children are born. It also comes packaged with other useful tools, including the "Bluff-O-Meter," the "Germ-O-Meter," and my personal favorite, the "Ignorator." The Ignorator allows us to hear our children's shouts, screams and other alarming sounds as so much family "elevator music." We moms all too often hurtle to the room that was the source of these violent sounds, expecting bloody mayhem, but all we discover are the puzzled looks of children, telling us that they are "just playing."

Anyway, the MotherFilter listening device is easy to use. When a child comes running to you breathlessly to report: "Mom! Come quick! Elvis fell down in the yard on an upside-down skate and he's GUSHING BLOOD all over the place! He probably needs to go to the emergency room and may never walk again!" it will alert you that Elvis tripped and fell and that, using a microscope, you might detect superficial scraping of the epidermis.

Ironically, the older kids get, especially boys, and the more their vocabularies should expand, the more limited their speech patterns become. You'd think that the nation was in the throes of a dire syllable shortage. They may be reading Dickens's *Tale of Two Cities* in school, but at home their responses to your inquiries about their health, happiness and welfare are generally met with any of the following:

A. "Whatever."
B. "Sorta."
C. "Yeah."
D. "What's for dinner?"
E. "Like maybe."
F. "Huh?"
G. "No way!"

H. "What did you say is for dinner?"

And, the perennial favorite,
I. "That's totally unfair!"

Perhaps it's the stress of being the generation after Generation X. Maybe our kids feel, on a subconscious level, that since only two letters remain in the entire alphabet to describe their generation, with neither letter particularly lending itself to a whole lot of linguistic variety, that they might as well not bother to say a whole lot.

Of course, kids may not fear that there is a syllable shortage—they may have been taught to recycle their words, along with their glass, paper, and aluminum. It wouldn't surprise me if their teachers have taught them that uttering sentences with more than ten words somehow hurts the Brazilian rain forest, because if there's anything that kids are learning about in school these days, it's about the rain forest. No matter what grade my kids are in, they're still learning about the ecosystem and endangered species. They've never heard of John Adams or Madame Curie in school, but they have all voted that Ben and Jerry should receive the Congressional Medal of Honor for using dioxin-free ice cream cartons.

One year at back-to-school night, I asked a teacher about this.

"Excuse me, I realize that you are a teacher and I am but a lowly parent, but can you explain to me how many more years the kids will be majoring in wetlands studies?"

"Some of us think that environmental studies are important," the teacher zinged back at me, the lowly parent.

"Yes, I agree, and believe me, we are scrupulous about recycling at home, but what about other science subjects, like astronomy? Isn't it time they learned that Pluto is more than just a Disney character?"

"When the planets begin to suffer ecological imbalance, we'll talk," said the teacher to me, the lowly parent.

It's ironic, though, that even kids who are firmly committed to the idea that recycling is the single most critical issue facing our nation in the new millennium have no trouble wasting other resources. Show me a kid who remembers to turn off the light switch when leaving a room and I'll show you a kid who learned to do it by means of a cattle prod. Our kids must think we run a Motel 6—they always leave the light on for you.

In the kids' defense, though, they do seem to be concerned about wasting water. They display this concern by refusing to bathe, wash their hands, or flush the toilet.

This is why all mothers—especially mothers of boys—do two things automatically when entering a bathroom. They flush the toilet and turn off the light. They don't even bother to look first—it's a conditioned reflex.

In truth, boys are far more likely to ration words than girls are. You can see this clearly if you overhear males and females using the telephone. Males use the phone as a means of nonelectronic data transfer. To a guy, the concept of a call just to "chat" is about as foreign as the idea of going to see a Fellini film. A typical guy conversation goes like this:

"Hey!"

"Yo!"

"Didja figure out how to download that program?"

"Yeah, no sweat!"

"Okay."

"Later."

And they hang up! Just like that! Maybe they think they're being charged by the word, but for whatever reason, guys like to get on and off the phone as fast as possible. Not so girls, who have much to say at every age. It begins when we put the Fisher-Price toy telephone in their chubby hands when they are only fourteen months old. They consider this an invitation to let loose a volley of conversation, opinion, gossip and stream of consciousness that sometimes lasts a lifetime. One Monday after school I asked my daughter to tell me about her day. She didn't finish telling me until the following Thursday.

My daughter is not unique in this regard. She has firm opinions and philosophies on every topic, and she began forming them as quickly as she formed her sentences at the age of two. Once, exasperated by the shenanigans of her brothers, I sighed and said rhetorically, "I just don't know what to say about that anymore." My then 4-year-old pundit said, "Well, I know what to say about it!" and issued forth a lengthy diatribe against her brothers' antics. Of all the comments I have received about my daughter, the most popular and recurring one is, "She certainly has a mighty command of the language for a girl her age, doesn't she?"

Girls are probably the main reason why the nation has been riled by so many area code splits lately. Really, we need new area codes not to accommodate the additional cell phone and modem connections, but to satisfy every teenage girl's inalienable right to get her own phone line. Parents are willing to spring for the extra lines as a ransom payment to get back their phones. Once they hit a certain age (though my daughter hit it about ten years earlier than the norm), girls' emotional stability depends on their freedom to describe in excruciating detail every microsecond of their day. They will start a call to tell their best friend about how every hair on their heads mutinied against them that morning, which ruined—totally—

their entire day by 7:30 a.m., leading to a migraine headache, causing them to be late for first period class, resulting in some sniggering on the part of their classmates, who obviously were laughing about the wayward strands of hair, and this of course led to 476 other traumatic insults to their psyche that day, each of which must be revisited closely to ensure that no further insults were missed. A friend of mine once timed her daughter on the phone. The mother clocked her daughter at more than 1,200 words per minute, but when she noticed her daughter turning blue, she was forced to interrupt the phone call to remind her daughter to breathe.

At least in those cases, the girls were somewhat articulate, if not a little overwrought. Too often, I'm left wondering how kids can even understand one another. Waiting in line at the market next to a trio of teenage girls, I overheard this conversation:

"So, he's like, not totally weird."

"So, you're like, dating him?"

"He's totally, y'know, kinda cool."

"He has a friend who's totally, like, whatever. His hair isn't that gross. I think I'll date him."

"Well, yeah! I mean, like, why not?"

"Yeah, like, if his hair isn't that gross! I hate gross hair!"

"Majorly!"

Now does this, like, majorly inspire confidence in tomorrow's youth, or like, whatever?

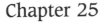

Chapter 25

Very Married

I realized that my husband and I had a problem in our relationship when we embraced spontaneously in the kitchen.

The problem wasn't the embrace; it was the fact that it induced a state of paralytic shock among our children. One minute they were elbowing one another to be the first to grab the new bag of Oreos, the next they had frozen in time, looking ready to ship off to Madame Tusaud's Wax Museum. My husband and I waved our hands repeatedly in front of their eyes, but they didn't blink or move for several moments.

"We've got to do this more often," the father of my children said.

"I would agree," I said.

Then, suddenly realizing that they had been left out, the two youngest unfroze themselves, darted towards us, and turned our embrace into a communal huddle. Then, my husband kissed me.

"YUUUUKKK!" our daughter groaned. "Daddy kissed Mommy on the LIPS! Oooohoooo! Did you see that?"

Our oldest son walked away in disgust. The others stayed, transfixed by the alarming display.

"Mommy, didn't you used to think it was disgusting to kiss on the lips?" our daughter asked.

"Yes, when I was your age."

"Did you get over it when you got married?"

"Well, DUH! Of course she did!" said another child, smirking.

All the magazines (well, perhaps not the *Journal of Accountancy* or *Candy and Nut Wholesaler*) regale women with the need to preserve the romantic side of their relationships with their husbands after they become parents. They give all kinds of unrealistic suggestions, such as "weekend getaways" without the kids. They don't realize that the zaniest, most impetuously romantic thing you may have managed to do with your husband in the past six months is to send him an instant message on his e-mail at work. They don't realize that you have been trying to get an appointment with your spouse for three weeks to discuss the leaking roof and neither of you has yet managed to find an open spot on your calendars. And they assume that the National Guard is just hanging around with nothing better to do than await your call inviting them to babysit your truculent troops while you rekindle the light of love at some beachside resort. There, you will have contests to see who can go longer before saying things like, "Wasn't it cute when Winston Salem pulled out his loose tooth at your mother's surprise party and bled on her brand-new white carpet?"

Sometime after the era of Long Moonlit Walks on the Beach but before the era of Did You Remember to Take Your

Metamucil? is the epoch of Parenthood. During this prolonged period, the marriage relationship metamorphoses into a whirlwind of parenting tasks: diapering, feeding, bathing, block-building and wiping peas and half-cut grapes off the floor. Sure, it progresses, to another whirlwind of weekend sports tryouts, ballet lessons, and evenings supervising homework, when you wrack your brain trying to remember the difference between congruent and adjacent angles.

Parents must not give up the struggle to reclaim romance. You'll know it's time to reignite the light of love when you start thinking of yourself as "dressed up" just because you removed the glow-in-the-dark Mickey Mouse bandage from your finger and ran a baby powder-scented diaper wipe along your forearms and behind the earlobes.

Displays of love and affection, like our madcap kitchen embrace, help remind us that we parents are more than just meal tickets and shuttle services for our kids. The first time we went out to dinner after one of our children was born, we chose a neighborhood restaurant for a quiet, romantic evening.

At the next table, some kindly grandparents were trying to restrain their grandchildren from banging on the bread plates with their water glasses and performing other antics that we could have witnessed at home for free. I didn't mean to shoot them a withering look, but I suppose I did, since I heard the grandmother say, "Now, now, Wilhelm and Petra, this nice couple didn't leave their own children at home to come here and listen to you carry on."

Damn straight, I thought, and beckoned the waitperson to show us to another table.

Truth to tell, we have managed to get away for some weekends, just the two of us. We spend more time planning these rendezvous than we actually spend away from home, since the logistical arrangements can take more time than the Pentagon needs to map out a surprise attack on an enemy country. It can take nearly all day to type out instructions about everyone's schedule and eating peculiarities, a document only slightly less detailed than the federal tax code. This is an excerpt from my most recent instruction list:

"Packing lunches: Make one peanut butter and jelly; two American cheese on bagels, and one jelly only on pumpernickel. Don't forget juice and chocolate milk boxes and fruit-rolls. Kids will tell you who gets what...

Dinner: Remember to put soy sauce, tomato sauce and ketchup on the table for the spaghetti, since everyone likes a different topping. Don't put green beans, or any other green foods, on same plate as pasta, or insurrection will ensue. Only pour orange juice without pulp, since the sight of pulp makes one child break out in hives. . .

Bedtime: Take out both Star Wars and Elmo toothpastes, since they don't all like the same type. Story time should begin no later than 7:30 or the little ones will stay up too late to wake up in time for school the next day. . .

Play dates: See attached list ("Schedule C") of play dates and phone numbers. Dates have been scheduled to ensure no more than two kids in the house at any given time. . ."

Now you would think that the caretakers would appreciate my thoroughness and thoughtfulness. Most do, except my mother, who waves the list in front of me and says, "No wonder you need a vacation! The way you cater to their every whim, it's disgraceful! When you were growing up, I put one dinner on the table, and if you were hungry you'd better eat it. That's what I'm going to do. This is absurd."

As usual, Mom was right, and I felt duly humbled.

Besides, I wouldn't be there when the mutiny began.

I recruit Mom for her tour of duty after the National Guard informs me it has higher priorities than my vacation. I also call in-laws, siblings, and friends whose relationships I feel can withstand the stress of caring for our children for a few days. I divvy up the baby-sitting into reasonable blocks of only four hours each to prevent battle fatigue.

Still, given her strong constitution and penchant for martyrdom, Mom gets the biggest hunk of time on duty and the honor of that last night in the house. When I call her from our picturesque little village several hours away from home to see how things are going, I use my most ingratiating tone of voice, just short of cloying. I can't take the chance that she will bolt.

"Hiya Mom! How're you doing? Everybody behaving?"

"'Behaving' is a neutral word. When did you say you're coming back?"

"Do you need me to speak to anybody?"

"No, no, you two just enjoy yourselves. I'll survive. You did say 4:00 tomorrow, didn't you? I have an appointment at 5:00 sharp."

"Uh, sure, Mom. Are they giving you a hard time?"

"No, not really." She sighs. This is not just any sigh. This is a classic Jewish mother sigh, with a history dating back thousands of years to when the Jews wandered in the desert for forty years without managing to find even one decent place for Chinese takeout. As such, it has been honed to guilt-inspiring perfection, and it speaks volumes. It is a sigh that has made Phillip Roth and Jackie Mason very rich men. In this particular case, though, it means, "I'm doing this as another in a series of ongoing sacrifices for you because I love you so much, so I fully expect that you will take care of me in my old age and not stick me in a nursing home. God knows I will have earned that right." The sigh is a tough act to follow.

When we do arrive home, not a minute before 4:00, Mom will be waiting at the door, overnight bag in hand. She won't even stay long enough for me to give her a little basket of hotel shampoos and soaps that I gathered especially for her.

"Seeya later," she will say. "I'm outta here."

During our weekend escapes, my husband and I revel in our time alone. With practice, we manage to talk about things that have nothing to do with disciplinary strategies, parent-teacher conferences or who can rearrange his or her schedule to attend the school science fair, where our proud young scientist will display his experiment on gingivitis. (This was my idea, since the materials were readily accessible.) We can even talk about current events, read aloud to each other, and revisit early dreams and desires for our life together. But I think what refreshes us most is that we can do all this for two solid days without anyone interrupting us.

We can saunter about in the evening, drop in on a jazz club or elegant restaurant where they play "Strangers in the Night" and contemplate the universe.

And of course, with no homework to supervise, no fights to mediate, we have plenty of time for those long walks on the beach and romantic interludes. It's then that I thank the Almighty for granting me a wonderful husband who can't see past his nose without his glasses. Between his near-sightedness and the Almighty's other great invention, darkness, the dear man still has no idea what four pregnancies have done to my body.

And I vow that once we come home, we will try to make those kitchen embraces frequent enough to avoid any future incidents of paralytic shock among our children.

Chapter 26

What the %$#@*& Happened to Good Manners?

My sons' registration forms to join the baseball league included the following disclaimer:

"The staff of the Brazen Bats Baseball League will not tolerate displays of unruly, combative, foul-mouthed or other obnoxious behavior. Such behavior is the sole province of major league basketball, football and baseball teams and has no place in youth league games. Determination of whether behavior is obnoxious is left to the sole discretion of the coaches, and the finding of such behavior will result in immediate removal from the game."

Mind you, this disclaimer wasn't aimed at the kids playing in the league. It was aimed at the *parents*. For some reason, American parents have more invested in their kids' athletic achievement than they do in all their mutual funds, 401Ks and IRAs combined. This is not true in Europe, however, where, I have heard, parents only show up at their kids' sporting matches if the spirit moves them. But west of the Atlantic, youth sports have become frighteningly serious business. Parents evaluate each referee's call in greater depth than they do decisions made by the United States Supreme Court on prayer in schools and states' rights.

At a basketball game we once attended, drama quickly ensued after the referee blew his whistle and did that funny pantomime thing with his hands, indicating some infraction of the game rules.

"Whaddaya mean, he fouled the other team! What kind of @&$%!^ call is that!" a father shouted from the bench.

"Calm down. Just 'cause it was your kid doesn't mean the call was bad. Admit it, your kid should never have been a starter."

"MY KID!" the offended parent jumped up, knocking several other parents' cell phones to the ground. "What about YOUR KID? You call that DEFENSE?"

Now, mind you, the kid who committed the foul had already forgotten about it and had raced back to the other side of the court, where he successfully blocked a basket by the opposing team. The kid looked to see if his parents were watching his moment of glory, but he did not see them. That was because his mother and father had left the gymnasium, frothing at the mouth, to call their attorney, highly regarded in the field of civil rights law, to press charges against the referee, the coach, the league, the school hosting the game, and the manufacturers of the basketball. In their view, if this basketball had been constructed safely, complete with foul-locks, it would never have malfunctioned, flying off track from their child's arms to foul a player from the opposing team.

Don't get me wrong. It's not that I don't understand a passion for sports. Believe me, I know what it's like to try to gather the males in the family for dinner when the Lakers are down by two at the end of the third quarter. My husband will say, "Okay, okay, just another five minutes!" (This equates to at least seven in dog years.)

But ah, how I long for those halcyon days when the kids' sports were...just games! Last baseball season (my calendar currently being divided neatly into baseball, soccer, basketball and hockey seasons), we attended one unforgettable game where a boy touched home plate nanoseconds after the baseball had arrived there. When the referee called the boy out, his mother suffered acute apoplexy.

This woman cried, cursed and generally provided great entertainment for the rest of us. "My son will need years of therapy because of this!" she screamed to the referee on the field, her emotional juggernaut probably setting the entire women's movement back fifty years. Poor kid! I thought. He'll need therapy, all right, but it won't be because of the referee's call.

Of course, the mother may have reacted that violently because she may have been among the growing legions of parents shelling out oodles of cash on private lessons to bolster her kid's pitching and batting ability. You'd think they were all Soviet gymnasts training for the Olympics, the way parents make these kids train from the age of three just so that one day, they can beat another team of nine-year-olds in a basketball game on a Saturday afternoon in a sweaty school gymnasium. And from there? Who knows? Nike endorsements, Wheaties boxes, and the glory of a career where you're history at thirty-five.

Even the *Los Angeles Times* has reported on families (not dotcom wealthy families, either) who have forked over enough money to pay for four years' tuition at Harvard plus a year or two of grad school and spending it on...Little League enrichment! Private coaches, state-of-the-art bats, balls, hockey sticks, tournament fees, gilded cleats, you name it, these parents are paying for it. Certainly they want to see that they're getting their money's worth.

My boys play in Little League too, but the only extra expense I'm willing to incur over and above the team fees is a few dollars at the little glucose-mobile parked on the street just behind home plate, where I buy everyone soda and ice cream bars after the game.

Besides, I don't know that extra lessons would help my kids. One son became so bored during a soccer game, even though he was the goalie, that he amused himself by hanging from his knees upside down from the goal post. He soon became lost in his own thoughts, which is where I can usually find him, and was completely oblivious to the fact that both teams were racing his way in a dramatic play unfolding before his backside. If he didn't get down and block the ball in the next five seconds, the opposing team would win. My oldest son, realizing what was at stake, screamed at him from the sidelines.

"WAKE UP, DUMMY! The ball's coming! IDIOT! WAKE UP! WAKE UP!" He could hardly contain himself, and I thought he was about to run onto the field personally to block the ball.

My son in the black and white soccer uniform instantly responded to this familiar brotherly clarion call. As he swung himself down, his knees blocked the other team's ball. Inadvertently, he saved the game and became an instant hero. He was thrilled, and his father and I made much of his great play, while we kept elbowing his older brother whenever he piped up that the team would have lost if not for HIS shout.

My youngest boy, during his freshman season on the

soccer field as a 5-year-old, was too busy most of the season holding hands with an adorable blond, blue-eyed girl he had decided to marry to pay much attention to the action surrounding him. Sometimes, though, the coach would yell, "Run! Run!" and my son duly obeyed. It looked like he was having fun.

My oldest son takes sports the most seriously in our family. He lives for the sports section of the newspaper, and knows the names and parole dates of thousands of ballplayers. He also seems to have some kind of inside track on who's about to be traded for whom, as well as details of the players' new mega-buck contracts. (Funny, though, how he has a hard time remembering to put on his orthodontic gear at night.) He is enormously proud of his shelf full of Little League trophies, which are the only things in his room he cleans willingly.

Participating in sports has done for him what we hoped it would: It has taught him how to lose without suffering what sports medicine physicians call Victorus Almostus. Symptoms of this ailment are appropriately athletic, and include flying off the handle, rushing to judgment and jumping to conclusions about the referee's partiality to the opposing team.

So far, my daughter has shown little interest in sports, though I will heartily encourage it. I know from personal experience what it's like to stand against the schoolyard fence and hear the captain of the other team looking at the last two rejects from the class and say with a pained expression, "Oh all right, I'll take Judy."

I don't know what drives parents to devote their lives to sculpt their kids to Hellenistic perfection. Call me old-fashioned, but it just seems to me that children should play sports for simple exercise, fun, and good sportsmanship.

If they don't learn it on the field, where will they learn it?

Certainly not from professional athletes. I once got a book from the library and read to my kids about Joe DiMaggio and other sports legends.

"See, boys?" I said to them, after reading about the distinctly gentlemanly behavior of many of these sports icons from a bygone era. "Not everyone used to feel that they needed to bite off the ears or strangle members of the opposing team when they got upset during a game."

"Didn't they even whack them with a hockey stick or baseball or something?"

"No, the fans wouldn't have tolerated it back then."

"Gee, that must've been in the really olden days. Nowadays, you get your own TV talk show by doing stuff like that."

"Yes, those were the days. It used to be, 'Choke a ref, go to prison.' Now it's 'Choke a ref, go on the talk show circuit.'"

"AND sign a book deal," added one son.

"Oh yes, I forgot. And sign a book deal."

Anyway, our family is gearing up for the next baseball season now, so we can kiss our Sundays goodbye for the next three months. And, just like that baseball registration flyer warned, my husband and I have got to watch our behavior on the field.

Last season, when my husband lit a cigar during a game, a frantic team representative rushed over to him.

"You can't smoke that here!" he barked at my husband.

"Why not? We're outside," my husband answered. "The smoke can't possibly bother anyone. I'm all the way against the fence."

"You don't get it," the team rep said, shaking his head and ignoring the fracas that had just erupted between parents arguing over the legality of a stolen third base. "It sets a bad example for the children!"

Chapter 27

The 700 Habits of Highly Defective Parents

(Don't Try These at Home)

Not sure about your skills as a mom? No sweat! Just go to any bookstore or troll the on-line aisles of a dotcom bookseller, and you are sure to find a title tailored specifically for you. And I do mean specifically. In fact, on a recent book-buying junket, I found so many titles dealing with the most picayune child-rearing concerns, I am certain that those publishers must have cut a sweet deal with bookshelf manufacturers.

Gone are the days when responsible parents could get all the child-rearing wisdom they needed from Dr. Spock's *Baby and Child Care*, and the occasional coffee-klatch with another parent or a clergyman. Now, even pregnancy books are specialized, with titles such as, *What to Eat During Your Fourth Month of Pregnancy*; *Feng Shui, Baby and Me*; and a 450-page book titled *Everything You Need to Know About Your Baby from Conception to Sixteen Weeks Gestation*. The publisher is no doubt rushing the sequel to market now, so as not to leave expectant mothers in their fifth month or later hanging in suspense.

Child guidance experts have kept themselves plenty busy penning books to help parents deal with every eventuality. Although I had gone in search of some general parenting tips, no such thing exists anymore. I had no idea that today's parents needed so much advice until I saw what was out there. Some of the more remarkable titles I found include:

Raising Your Brave, Kind Yet Explosively Tempered Child; *I Hate You Mom, but Can You Drive Me to the Movies?*; *Raising Your Right-Brained Child in a Pacific Standard Time Zone*; *Don't Be Afraid to Discipline Your Hyperactive, Lactose-Intolerant Child*; *The Secret Emotional Life of Your Pet Gerbil*; and *Who Moved My Cheez-Whiz? Strategies for Junk-Food-Addicted Parents*.

These days, the topic of mothers and sons is hotter than jalapeño pepper salsa. Dozens of books instruct us to hug our sons more to make them into masculine, yet sensitive men. We should support their innate masculinity, the books say. We should support their emotional fragility. We should acknowledge how hard it is to be a boy in this society where gender issues have become so complex. This is all true. But in addition, I think we should also do something even more fundamental for our boys: put up a basketball hoop in the backyard, buy them a slushie at least once a week at the local mini-mart, and don't make them shower more than three times a week.

Personally, I already have a whole slew of child-rearing titles at home. I have even read some of them and attempted a few of the strategies. Despite this, none of my children has ever been removed from my custody by the authorities. But then again, the books on my shelf were not targeted to my particular situations. If they had been, I surely would have read titles such as *Healthy Menus for Kids Who Eat Only Raw Noodles and Ketchup* and *How to Rear Children Who Know Infinitely More Than You Do.*

That's the real tar baby in this whole child-rearing literature racket. No matter how much the authors tailor their work to specific kinds of kids, the gambits never quite work for you.

"I'm never buying another child development book again," huffed my friend Mary when we spoke about the issue. "Sure, the methods always work great on paper and with someone else's kids, but when I try them at home, the kids just look at me funny and ask, 'Are you trying to improve our family life again?' I've had enough advice."

I know what Mary means. Many times I've run out to buy books that my friends said were "must-reads." These have included *Raising Boys to Lower the Toilet Seat* and *1,002 Ways to Get Your Daughter off the Phone.* This niche marketing is pretty clever, since many of the titles fairly scream out for sequels. So, one shelf in the bookstore where I shopped began with the book, *What Your Sixth-Grader Must Know*, which burgeoned into a series focused on every grade from graduate school all the way down to *What Every Six-Week Fetus Needs to Know.*

We already live in a world of information overload. I want my advice simple and straightforward. But many of these advice books are chock full of charts and gimmicks that you've got to individualize for each kid. Housework charts, good behavior charts, homework charts, healthy eating charts. There were so many graphs and charts in one opus that I thought I was reading an actuarial table.

I've also attended numerous lectures on how to raise good children. I usually sit up front, afraid to miss any choice suggestions. One time the speaker was a young mother and educator, who told us that some of her best advice had come from a renowned educator who had raised eight kids successfully.

According to widely circulated reports, all were credits to the human race. How had he done it? the speaker had asked him one day.

He looked at her a moment, not saying anything, then just shrugged his shoulders and began to walk away.

"Wait! You didn't answer my question!" the woman persisted. "You've got valuable information that the world needs! Can't you tell me something about your method for raising great children? What did you and your wife do? Or what didn't you do?"

Again he shrugged his response, though in a very philosophical pose, and again she doggedly pursued him. Finally, seeing that he couldn't escape the grilling, he said, "Just don't get personally involved."

As she related this story, we were all slack-jawed. While everyone and their brother-in-law insist that we parents must be intricately involved with every facet of our children's lives, along comes this guy with a bunch of well-adjusted kids all grown up and the sum total of his advice is basically, "hands off."

She said that this had come as an extraordinary revelation to her, and that she had co-opted this philosophy successfully. (This didn't include the time, however, that one of her youngsters had decided to shear all her siblings' hair with a manicure scissors.)

I considered this new aloof parenting tactic. Get some emotional distance from the kids. Yes, that just might be the ticket. But this didn't work either, as I quickly learned at home.

"MOMMY! He called me STUPID!"

I would not get embroiled this time. I would not get personally involved. I continued to slice vegetables for soup. For no particular reason, I began humming Brahms Hungarian Dance no. 5 in G Minor.

"DID YOU HEAR ME, MOMMY?" my daughter repeated, fortissimo. This is a girl who specialized in living in a state of perpetual outrage.

"Oh, did you say something, darling? Well, of course you're not stupid, so just ignore it."

I thought this was brilliant. Yes, this would work. Stay calm, above the fray.

However, my daughter began to have what we politely call a meltdown due to my callous indifference, thwarting my efforts to remain parentally detached. Well, I would try it with the boys, I told myself as I reverted to my old, sympathetic parenting style.

In my career as a mother, I've tried more child-rearing schemes than I have dinner recipes. I've "reflected" my children's feelings back to them to encourage communication. This worked beautifully on some kids, and, buoyed by my triumph, I tried it on another. That's when my winning streak ended. When I "reflected" back to this child, he cocked his head slightly and inquired, "You feeling okay, Mom?"

I've drawn up "star charts" to encourage good behavior. These never worked for me, either, since my kids would often sneak into the room where I kept the charts and fill in entire rows with stars, "proving" that they had earned the grand prize of a trip to the toy store.

When I had exhausted my pool of "positive" approaches, I tried to restore order in the family with a "tough love" approach. I've tried ignoring fights, mediating fights, and putting myself in time-out. I suppose I should have read *Wednesdays with Winston*, about a kindly old man who came over each week to baby-sit and share his philosophy of life while the mother made a beeline out of the house for a few hours by herself.

Sometimes, I end up sounding more like a bad television cop show than any sage child-rearing tome when I'm trying to discipline my kids. Running to a room where the kids have come to blows, I have actually said, "Don't anybody move— just put your hands up and no one gets hurt!"

And so, when they insist on reenacting scenes from *America's Most Wanted*, I end up as (who else?) Judge Judy, enforcing "the long arm of the Ma." I need to do this when my sons decide the only thing they can think of to put off their homework any longer is to take turns putting their sister in a full headlock and then ricocheting around the house with invisible "Star Wars" weaponry, speaking Jedi. Of course, it is only fun to do this in the one room in the house where I have dared to display breakable objects.

At times like these, I don't run for the child-rearing books. Who has time to reference the chapter on *Testosterone Poisoning in the Home*? Instead, I go into June Cleaver mode: "I'm going to tell your father about this!" I warn the great unwashed, who suddenly recover their hearing. (Happily, I remember not to call my husband "Ward" when he comes home. And I neglect to wear pearls when I vaccuum.)

I'm not surprised that military academies sprang up before our nation was assaulted with this avalanche of parenting advice. In fact, watching boys at "play" I understand the entire concept of the military in a way I never could when I was young and pasted bumper stickers on my car that said, "One nuclear bomb can ruin your whole day." Now I realize that boys need structure, lots of it, and who better to dole it out than men wearing uniforms with ammunition belts?

This may also explain the slew of books all about boys, none of which I have bothered to read. First of all, I'd need a different book for each son, since the books are so specific. Maybe, if those New Age baby name books had been published back when I was shopping for names, it would have been easier. One such book I saw encouraged parents to bestow names with cultural and symbolic meaning. These names might also instill wonderful, peaceful personal qualities and traits in the child, according to the book's rhapsodic authors. To accomplish this, parents are instructed to take names, or parts of names, from Swahili, Nibaw and the Ibo languages, among others, to create a conceptually beautiful, yet gender-neutral name. But it's too late to start calling my kids Oriba Alka, or Kamata, or even Montel.

For my money, the most relevant book I saw in the bookstore that day was *The 700 Habits of Highly Defective Parents.* This book, at least, seemed to offer something for everyone.

Chapter 28

Practicing Safe Parenting

As my husband and I prepared to go out for the evening, we quickly went through our checklist of safety procedures. As usual, it took us longer to safeguard our children against what was INSIDE the house rather than from what was OUTSIDE:

"V-chip activated on the TV?"

"Check!"

"Internet filter installed on the computer?"

"Check!"

"Cell phone charged?"

"Check!"

"Pager on?"

"Check!"

"Doors locked?"

"No, we haven't left yet."

"Ooops. Right."

"Emergency numbers on the fridge?"

"Check!"

"Got any cash on you?"

"I thought you had money! Oh well, there's always plastic. I think we're ready, let's go!"

Now when I was growing up, all responsible parents had to do before they went out was hire a sitter, make sure there were plenty of good eats in the pantry, leave an emergency phone number handy and lock the doors. Of course, in those days, our most high-tech possession was an electric toothbrush—a revolutionary advance in dental hygiene at that time.

Nowadays, though, we are slaves to high-tech, at home as well as at work. We even need technology to help us practice safe parenting. Call me old-fashioned, but when I go out to dinner with my husband I would like my biggest worry to be that we will accidentally order "pasketti" instead of "spaghetti." I don't want to think that under a babysitter's less than vigilant eye, my kids might uncover a full menu of sexual antics and perversity through an accidental click of the computer mouse.

This danger became apparent to me when my oldest son announced that he had established his own e-mail account. I realized then that I had to get a filter for our Internet access—within the hour, if possible. Now, the site that sponsors our Web filter also offers us a steady diet of heavy-duty theological messages. And, even though it's not our particular theology, I far prefer him studying Saint Vincent than all of Victoria's secrets. After all, if I wanted my kids to have a portal to pornography via the World Wide Web, I'd drop them off at the local library.

Frankly, I love the research and shopping opportunities that the Internet affords and can't see doing without it, so I'm grateful for the filtering devices. What I don't understand, though, is why parents fritter their time away, struggling to decipher the crazy alphabet soup of parental warnings in the television guides. Who can figure this out? They've got eighty-seven different combinations of letters and numbers on the order of: "F.B.N.T." (this show is okay for your 5-year-old but not your 3-year-old); "13 N. 11.5" (this show is okay for your 13-year-old but not your 11 1/2-year-old); and "A.W.H." (all ages will hate this). Of course, this rating guide bears little resemblance to the movie ratings. That would have been too simple.

We have bypassed this problem in our house by basically using the television as a video monitor. We make exceptions, such as for NBA play-offs, the hourly Christmastime showings of *It's a Wonderful Life*, and other special events, such as a NASA space shuttle landing on a distant planet. I can't see any evidence that my kids have been materially deprived by this. The last thing I need is for them to watch shows where big-mouth cynical kids always know more than their milquetoast, discipline-impaired parents. Besides, the experts have agreed that kids who watch an average of two hours of television a day not only see seven bazillion murders a year, but also two trillion couples peeling off their clothes and tumbling in the sack together before they've even exchanged pager numbers.

So for TV watchers across the land, the V-chip is as necessary an accompaniment to an evening's entertainment as the Cajun-spiced potato chip. And other technology devices can be very useful also. For example, a motion detector can not only alert you to prowlers on your property, it can also tell you if your teenager has awakened by lunchtime. Extremely mobile kids can reach their equally extremely mobile parents on the cell phone or by pager. And even voice mail message systems have helped expedite parenting chores. I read about one really bottom-line executive parent who installed the following message system on her private line at work:

"Hi. You've reached Mom. Your call is very important to me, so please listen to the following options carefully. If you lost your homework, press one. If you have a headache at school and believe you must be picked up, press two. If you cannot find a pair of clean jeans, press three, and you will be connected with the first available dry cleaner. . ."

Some working parents have installed video cameras in their homes to snoop on their young children's caretakers. This is fine if you are parenting by proxy, I suppose, but I've been thinking of installing one in the kitchen. That way, the next time I discover that the ice cream is all gone, and every single child swears "It wasn't me!" I can replay the videotape as my evening's entertainment and catch the culprit. I may even go one better and, to avoid that last-minute stampede to the dinner table, do what the banks have done and install a security door leading to the kitchen. The soon-to-be patented "Mom's Meal Moat" will enable access to only one customer at a time, and only when the green light is on.

Yes, video monitors are ubiquitous, and I suppose that once we get used to the idea that our images are unfairly preserved on grainy film, making us look heavier and paler than we are, our society may be made safer by having them.

But what about all those blasted television sets that they've put in supermarkets, doctors' offices, even cars, for Pete's sake? This kind of emotional sedation of our kids may seem clever in the short run. It gives the doctors an easy out for having kept our sick kids sitting for forty-five minutes in the waiting room while we are stuck thumbing through last year's *Physician Four-Iron* magazine. And in the supermarket, the televisions deflect our kids' attention from the candy aisle. But, given this steady drumbeat of video images, no one should be mystified by our national epidemic of attention deficit disorder. What do you expect when kids have never learned to live without entertainment for longer than two minutes at a stretch?

Anyway, most people know that despite what some politicians claim, the real "digital divide" in this country isn't between the rich and poor: It's between kids and their parents. Today's kids, even without the benefit of any computer classes, still seem to know innately how to write software programs and design their own Web pages. I've been stunned to come back to my computer and find that my 6-year-old had changed my wallpaper and screen saver patterns and installed a new "Math Blaster" program. Meanwhile, I have been reduced to asking them for help to figure out the most elementary tasks, such as how to cut and paste from one document to the next. How do they know all this? The only thing I can guess is all that genetically engineered food they're eating must have some kind of "techie" vitamins in them. Of course, this same genetically engineered food may also explain why our teens are growing feet the size of Vermont, but I digress.

Still, I fear our hard-wired, electronic way of life can be taken too far. One night when I was tapping away at my laptop, I realized that it was suspiciously quiet in the house. I got up from my work and prowled around the house, where I discovered that my eldest son was trading designated hitters on his Internet-based Fantasy Baseball League. Another son was listening to the radio with a headset. My youngest boy was transfixed by a hand-held electronic game of Twenty-One, and my daughter was zoning out on her 357th viewing of one of her favorite Disney videos. We were all connected, but none of us to one another. I then put away my laptop, and walked around disconnecting everyone else from his or her game or device. I'm sure you can just imagine how my popularity soared.

That's why I think that, pagers, voice mail, V-chips and Internet filters aside, all parents should invest in some really low-tech gizmos to help them with their child-rearing. Here's my list of ten favorite low-tech devices, none of which requires batteries or warranty cards:

1. Kitchen timer—wind it for a set amount of time, say ten minutes, and have your kids compete to clean up their rooms in the allotted time span. Winners earn dessert. Losers get to try again.

2. Trash cans—introduce your children to them, pointing out that they don't have feet and therefore must be carried out to the alley.

3. Books—these have the benefits of portability and don't need batteries. They are interactive, as the words remain on the page but human eyes can scan over them and sometimes absorb their meaning. Can occasionally be educational.

4. Alarm clocks—useful for recalcitrant teens who believe that the Bill of Rights provides them the inalienable rights to life, liberty and the pursuit of REM mode till the day is half over.

5. Cutlery—one day, if you keep nagging, perhaps your children will actually use it.

6. Sweaters—a must for chilly days. Don't ever expect to see these articles of clothing again, though, especially if they are new or expensive. They will be swallowed up by that black hole known as the schoolyard.

7. Extra-Strength Pain Reliever—for those days when

chocolate truffles are unavailable and running away from home is not an option.

8. Slide locks on the bedroom door—can save a mom and dad from some embarrassing interruptions in the late hours of the evening and curtail psychiatric bills.

9. Monopoly—They say that the family that plays games together stays together. But this is only if you all take turns being Banker.

10. Grandma and Grandpa—the most cost-effective alternative to automated, digitized, and solar child-monitoring devices.

Sometimes, there's just no substitute for low-tech.

Chapter 29

Parental Paradoxes

When one of my kids is invited to sleep over at a friend's house, I do what all moms do: admonish him not to cause terminal damage to the family name. We would be horrified if, when our children were guests at another's home, they felt comfortable enough to act as if they were home, chewing with their mouths open and carrying on conversations from the bathroom with the door open.

So as a preemptive strike, we tell the host parent, "Please don't hesitate to call me if Jericho stirs up any trouble. I'll come right over and pick him up." And we go home and wait for the phone to ring. But usually it doesn't, and this leads us to Parental Paradox Number One: Our kids have split personalities. There is, of course, the personality we know best, the one that our children manifest by grabbing their siblings' attention with hockey sticks and glass-shattering shouts. And there is this other personality, one apparently molded through the secret use of behavioral modification tapes they listen to at bedtime. These tapes obviously are distributed by the most exclusive finishing schools in Europe, and help create the Professor Higgins counterpart to your usual Eliza Doolittle. Unfortunately for us moms, the Professor Higgins alter-ego only escapes from the Eliza Doolittle personality out of range of our hearing and sight. It's no wonder that when I really want to get my kids to behave at home, I say, "Can't you just pretend you're somewhere else?"

We mothers stream messages of civility on our round-the-clock, broadband mothering network twenty-four hours a day. Our figures have been ruined forever by these children, and we have lost decades of sleep catering to their every need in babyhood and beyond. Yet despite our heroic sacrifices, we are rarely granted an audience with this other, distinguished personality.

Instead, we learn about its existence through hearsay.

So when we pick up little Jericho at the end of the sleep-over, we are nonplused to hear the host child's mother say, "My goodness, what excellent manners your child has! I've never had such a well-mannered, polite child as a guest before!" And just as you turn around to see which mother behind you is being addressed, you realize it's you. Be still, my beating heart! I have often thought, wouldn't it be nice to see this well-bred, refined child in action, to verify his existence? I for one would be thrilled to see this person come alive, and express his true inner animated self when no one is looking, like one of the toys in *Toy Story*. I think next time my kids are invited elsewhere, I will ask the host parent if I can install a small surveillance camera in their house to capture the kid on film using a napkin instead of a shirt sleeve. Now that's a video I would watch over and over.

It's no big surprise that the old television program, *Kids Say the Darndest Things*, has been reprised. Who can resist laughing at the hilariously frank perceptions of kids? In fact, kids' often-brutal honesty leads us to Parental Paradox Number Two: When we teach our kids that honesty is the best policy, it can backfire on us.

Let's say you have guests over for dinner, your old friend Tom, whom you haven't seen in a year or two, his new wife, Elsa, and a business client. Count on your child to give a sideways glance at Tom, who is seated next to his wife, and sidle over to him, asking, "Weren't you married to Sally last time?" Or, facing your client, ask, "Did you forget to brush your teeth? They're really yellow." (Reality byte: One of my kids asked the "yellow teeth" question—of his dentist!)

You try to shoo the child away quickly, but the damage has been done. You can kiss your friendship with Tom and Elsa goodbye, along with that new account.

As kids get older and more sophisticated, they know better than to tell the truth all the time. After all, the truth, unless you are a polished politician, has its consequences. The truth could get your kids into trouble. Let's say you have it on good authority that they watched some horrifying slasher flick while at a friend's house, despite your warnings expressly forbidding anything rated PG or higher in the alphabet. You ask the kid about it, and this is what he is likely to say:

Mom: "Charleston, did you really see *Ghoul's Night Out* over at Quedisha's house?"

Charleston: (whose expression conveys both fear and defiance) "Huh? Did we see *Ghouls Night Out*? No, uh, uh, we saw, um, what was it called again? Oh yeah! We saw *The Sound of Music*! Yeah, that's it, *The Sound of Music*."

We hope that one day our kids will fudge the truth only

to avoid hurting the feelings of others...or being bumped up into a higher tax bracket. (Just kidding, IRS!) Otherwise, it is possible that they may end up as career politicians. Depending on what the definition of the word "is" is.

Before I became a mom, a friend of mine who already was one told me, "Being a mother is a continual process of letting go." This sounded very wise to me, but it wasn't until I became a mom that I understood the existence of Parental Paradox Number Three: Just when we think we want our kids to be independent, we change our minds and cling to them for dear life.

When kids are very small, they like to congeal themselves to you. Some of mine used to burrow in so deep it seemed they were trying to get back inside. Small kids can remain affixed to us this way for several years, until the kindergarten teacher firmly says, "You really need to leave now, Mrs. Gruen." After one such dismissal, I spent the entire month of October hiding outside my son's preschool class, in case he began to cry for me. As moms, we want our kids to want us, but it still hurts when they scream or whimper once we do leave them for a while. Of course, togetherness has its limits. One mother I know was so desperate for a solo potty break she had to leave the state to avert yet another incident of voidus interruptus.

While our children's attachment to us is poignant, it can also be downright frustrating. From time to time, we moms have to separate from our children. And so in these early years motherhood is indeed a process of letting go, in this case, of trying to get the child to let go of you.

Many years later, when those same young tots have grown into teenagers with frighteningly autonomous lives, the roles are reversed: Now it is you, the mom, velcroing yourself to the kid, hoping that you will make his e-mail "Buddy List." You begin to think, but dare not say, "Don't go! Forgive me for all the times I made you bathe against your will and forbade you from watching morning cartoons. Just don't ride off into the sunset with that strange girl with the earrings in her eyebrow!"

Will we ever get it right, this dance of dependence and independence?

One night, I had to speak about a very serious and delicate topic with a particular child. I tried to explain, as sensitively and forthrightly as I could, that one of his grandparents was quite ill, and might not survive.

I didn't want to overtax my son, or give more information than needed, but I wanted to answer any and all questions he had. I was prepared for anything, or so I thought. This is when I discovered Parental Paradox Number Four: You may think that you understand your kids' thought processes, but you don't. Never underestimate the extent to which your children's reality is focused on the immediate, and is subject to rapid and unexpected twists.

That night, for example, I sensed that our talk was winding down, and that my son had ingested enough of what I had to explain. He had been appropriately somber during our discussion. I was ready to kiss him goodnight. But then he said, "Mom, can I ask you something?"

I looked at his pensive face and wondered what other elements of life and death he might want to ask about.

"Sure, honey, what is it?" I awaited a poignant moment in our discussion of the Big Issues of Life, one that would bond us closer for the rest of our days.

"Well," he began, looking kind of worried, "I accidentally sat on my retainer at school today and it broke. Are you going to get really mad at me?"

Every mother knows all about Parental Paradox Five: Even when we have been mothers for several years, we are still someone else's child. My own mother reminded me of this recently, when she came to watch the kids one evening.

"You can't go out with wet hair like that. You'll catch cold!" Mom said.

Like a lot of motherly commands, this one wasn't worth arguing over. If we had been in the Mojave Desert in August and Mom saw me trying to slip out of the tent with wet hair, she would stop me and insist that I dry it, lest I catch cold.

So I'm drying my hair, thinking about the fact that I'm staring down a big birthday soon, you know, the one that begins with a "Four" and ends with an "Oh," and I still can't leave the house until Mom says I can. Hair dry, I reemerge only to have Mom say (you can guess what's coming), "Where's your sweater? It's chilly outside!"

You would think that these kinds of episodes would give me more understanding and sympathy when my own kids insist that they aren't cold and I am foisting sweaters on them. But we moms can't help it. This is just genetic, and is proven by that old classic joke:

What's the definition of a sweater?

Answer: An article of clothing you wear when your mother is cold.

As a parent, you will devote years trying to mold your kids into fabulous adults. This takes hard work. First, you've got to eradicate bad habits from among your children's arsenal of behaviors and quirks. You've got to convince children that, contrary to what they have heard through the schoolyard grapevine, tossing dirty clothes into the hamper won't kill them, and neither will giving in during an argument. After years without progress, though, you may despair. You may even begin to understand why mothers in the animal kingdom often eat their young. (This is especially true of the mothers of adolescent animals.)

But hang in there! Parental Paradox Number Six is that just when you think all is lost, and worry that even when your kids are thirty-three years old you will still have to call them every morning at 6:30 to wake them up to go to work, they suddenly get it. They mature. Well, not enough for them to leave home, which we are not ready for in any case, but just enough to put a spring in our maternal step.

I have seen this phenomenon with my very eyes, and even called the Jet Propulsion Laboratory to report one such sighting. One night, my husband came home from work and found me on the living room couch, wringing my hands and weeping.

"What's wrong?" he asked in alarm.

"It's our eldest child..." I began, unsure if I could go on. It was so hard to get the words out. "He...*listened* the first time I told him to do something."

My husband dropped his briefcase on the floor and slumped down next to me on the couch. The color drained from his face. "What? Have you taken his temperature? Should we call the doctor? A therapist? What could be the matter with him? He was acting normally yesterday."

"I know!" I said. "I'd heard about such things happening, but I never thought it would happen to us!"

The next time one of our kids displayed this kind of behavior, I nearly trampled the poor kid with my enthusiasm and praise until he finally said, "It's okay Mom. You can stop now."

All moms can cite examples like this. The 4-year-old who's bursting out of industrial-sized diapers finally gets potty-trained. A kid who you predicted would need dentures by middle school finally realizes he ought to brush his teeth before he loses the ability to bite into any more hot dogs. The girl who finally understands that spending in excess of two hours a day on her hair can be hazardous to her health.

That's what we live for, we moms, these small moments of triumph that lead us to think, "I must be doing something right!"

And you know what? We are.

Afterword

A Note From Judy

We moms try to teach our children to say both "please" and "thank you" as a basic part of good manners. Now it is my turn to say both to you.

First, thank you for reading *Carpool Tunnel Syndrome*. I had a great time writing it, and I hope I succeeded in bringing smiles of recognition and laughter to you, my colleagues in motherhood. (Okay, okay, I also needed to get these stories down on paper—it was cheaper than therapy.)

If my stories resonated with you, I'd love to hear from you. You can write to me at the address below or email me at: judygruen@att.net.

And now for the "please." Remember the chapter *Culture Mulcher Mom*? (It's on page 92 in case you have very short-term memory.) Like most of the book, the anecdotes in this chapter are based in fact. I really did write those letters, make those calls, and admonish a stranger for his foul language in public. I know that I'm not alone in trying to take small steps to make our communities better, more wholesome places, for ourselves and for our children.

In a future project, I plan to highlight stories of other "cultural crusaders" who have made a difference in their hometowns. Have you or someone you know succeeded in getting offensive billboards removed from your neigborhood? Convinced a media outlet to stop running demeaning programming? Sponsored a TV-free week at your children's school?

Please send your letters or stories to:
Judy Gruen
Culture Mulcher Mom
c/o Heaven Ink Publishing
8847 Cattaraugus Avenue
Los Angeles, CA 90034.

You can also email me at: judygruen@att.net

Please make sure to include your full name, address, phone number and email address for verification.

I look forward to hearing from you!

Give the Gift of Laughter

Your mother, sisters, aunts, cousins & friends will love *Carpool Tunnel Syndrome*!

Check your leading bookstore or order here

❑ **YES!** I want _____ copies of *Carpool Tunnel Syndrome: Motherhood as Shuttle Diplomacy* at $12.95 each, plus $4 shipping and handling per book. (California residents, please add $1.07 sales tax for each book) U.S. funds only.

My check or money order for $_____ is enclosed.

Please charge my: ❑ VISA   ❑ MasterCard

Name_____

Address _____

City/State/Zip_____

Phone_____Fax_____

Email_____

Credit Card # _____/_____/_____/_____

Expiration date _____

Signature_____

Please make your check payable to:
Heaven Ink Publishing
8847 Cattaraugus Avenue
Los Angeles, CA 90034

heavenink@earthlink.net
www.heavenink.com

**Or call in your credit card order toll-free to:
1-800-836-1021**

Call or email us to ask about **quantity discounts** available to **groups, organizations** or for use in fundraising!

Give the Gift of Laughter

Your mother, sisters, aunts, cousins & friends will love *Carpool Tunnel Syndrome*!

₹◐

Check your leading bookstore or order here

❏YES! I want _____ copies of *Carpool Tunnel Syndrome: Motherhood as Shuttle Diplomacy* at $12.95 each, plus $4 shipping and handling per book. (California residents, please add $1.07 sales tax for each book) U.S. funds only.

My check or money order for $_____ is enclosed.

Please charge my: ❏ VISA   ❏ MasterCard

Name_____

Address _____

City/State/Zip_____

Phone_____Fax_____

Email_____

Credit Card # _____/_____/_____/_____

Expiration date _____

Signature_____

Please make your check payable to:
Heaven Ink Publishing
8847 Cattaraugus Avenue
Los Angeles, CA 90034

heavenink@earthlink.net
www.heavenink.com

Or call in your credit card order toll-free to:
1-800-836-1021

Call or email us to ask about
quantity discounts available to
groups, organizations
or for use in fundraising!